The beautiful works of the Reverend Mr. Stephen Duck, ... To which is prefixed, some account of his life and writings.

Stephen Duck

ECCO
PRINT EDITIONS

Gale ECCO Print Editions

Relive history with *Eighteenth Century Collections Online*, now available in print for the independent historian and collector. This series includes the most significant English-language and foreign-language works printed in Great Britain during the eighteenth century, and is organized in seven different subject areas including literature and language; medicine, science, and technology; and religion and philosophy. The collection also includes thousands of important works from the Americas.

The eighteenth century has been called "The Age of Enlightenment." It was a period of rapid advance in print culture and publishing, in world exploration, and in the rapid growth of science and technology – all of which had a profound impact on the political and cultural landscape. At the end of the century the American Revolution, French Revolution and Industrial Revolution, perhaps three of the most significant events in modern history, set in motion developments that eventually dominated world political, economic, and social life.

In a groundbreaking effort, Gale initiated a revolution of its own: digitization of epic proportions to preserve these invaluable works in the largest online archive of its kind. Contributions from major world libraries constitute over 175,000 original printed works. Scanned images of the actual pages, rather than transcriptions, recreate the works *as they first appeared.*

Now for the first time, these high-quality digital scans of original works are available via print-on-demand, making them readily accessible to libraries, students, independent scholars, and readers of all ages.

For our initial release we have created seven robust collections to form one the world's most comprehensive catalogs of 18th century works.

Initial Gale ECCO Print Editions collections include:

History and Geography

Rich in titles on English life and social history, this collection spans the world as it was known to eighteenth-century historians and explorers. Titles include a wealth of travel accounts and diaries, histories of nations from throughout the world, and maps and charts of a world that was still being discovered. Students of the War of American Independence will find fascinating accounts from the British side of conflict.

Social Science

Delve into what it was like to live during the eighteenth century by reading the first-hand accounts of everyday people, including city dwellers and farmers, businessmen and bankers, artisans and merchants, artists and their patrons, politicians and their constituents. Original texts make the American, French, and Industrial revolutions vividly contemporary.

Medicine, Science and Technology

Medical theory and practice of the 1700s developed rapidly, as is evidenced by the extensive collection, which includes descriptions of diseases, their conditions, and treatments. Books on science and technology, agriculture, military technology, natural philosophy, even cookbooks, are all contained here.

Literature and Language

Western literary study flows out of eighteenth-century works by Alexander Pope, Daniel Defoe, Henry Fielding, Frances Burney, Denis Diderot, Johann Gottfried Herder, Johann Wolfgang von Goethe, and others. Experience the birth of the modern novel, or compare the development of language using dictionaries and grammar discourses.

Religion and Philosophy

The Age of Enlightenment profoundly enriched religious and philosophical understanding and continues to influence present-day thinking. Works collected here include masterpieces by David Hume, Immanuel Kant, and Jean-Jacques Rousseau, as well as religious sermons and moral debates on the issues of the day, such as the slave trade. The Age of Reason saw conflict between Protestantism and Catholicism transformed into one between faith and logic -- a debate that continues in the twenty-first century.

Law and Reference

This collection reveals the history of English common law and Empire law in a vastly changing world of British expansion. Dominating the legal field is the *Commentaries of the Law of England* by Sir William Blackstone, which first appeared in 1765. Reference works such as almanacs and catalogues continue to educate us by revealing the day-to-day workings of society.

Fine Arts

The eighteenth-century fascination with Greek and Roman antiquity followed the systematic excavation of the ruins at Pompeii and Herculaneum in southern Italy; and after 1750 a neoclassical style dominated all artistic fields. The titles here trace developments in mostly English-language works on painting, sculpture, architecture, music, theater, and other disciplines. Instructional works on musical instruments, catalogs of art objects, comic operas, and more are also included.

The BiblioLife Network

This project was made possible in part by the BiblioLife Network (BLN), a project aimed at addressing some of the huge challenges facing book preservationists around the world. The BLN includes libraries, library networks, archives, subject matter experts, online communities and library service providers. We believe every book ever published should be available as a high-quality print reproduction; printed on-demand anywhere in the world. This insures the ongoing accessibility of the content and helps generate sustainable revenue for the libraries and organizations that work to preserve these important materials.

The following book is in the "public domain" and represents an authentic reproduction of the text as printed by the original publisher. While we have attempted to accurately maintain the integrity of the original work, there are sometimes problems with the original work or the micro-film from which the books were digitized. This can result in minor errors in reproduction. Possible imperfections include missing and blurred pages, poor pictures, markings and other reproduction issues beyond our control. Because this work is culturally important, we have made it available as part of our commitment to protecting, preserving, and promoting the world's literature.

GUIDE TO FOLD-OUTS MAPS and OVERSIZED IMAGES

The book you are reading was digitized from microfilm captured over the past thirty to forty years. Years after the creation of the original microfilm, the book was converted to digital files and made available in an online database.

In an online database, page images do not need to conform to the size restrictions found in a printed book. When converting these images back into a printed bound book, the page sizes are standardized in ways that maintain the detail of the original. For large images, such as fold-out maps, the original page image is split into two or more pages

Guidelines used to determine how to split the page image follows:

• Some images are split vertically; large images require vertical and horizontal splits.
• For horizontal splits, the content is split left to right.
• For vertical splits, the content is split from top to bottom.
• For both vertical and horizontal splits, the image is processed from top left to bottom right.

The BEAUTIFUL

WORKS

Of the REVEREND

Mr. STEPHEN DUCK,

(The *Wiltſhire* BARD:)

Who was many Years a poor Thieſher in a Barn,
at *Charleton* in the County of *Wilts*, at the Wages
of four Shillings and Six-pence *per* Week, 'till taken
Notice of by Her late Majeſty Queen CAROLINE;
who, on Account of his great Genius, gave him an
Apartment at *Kew*, near *Richmond*, in *Surry*, and a
Salary of Thirty Pounds *per Annum*; after which
he ſtudied the learned Languages, took Orders, and
is now a dignified Clergyman.

To which is prefixed,

SOME

ACCOUNT

OF HIS

LIFE and WRITINGS.

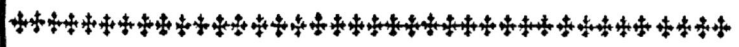

✠✠✠✠✠✠✠✠✠✠✠✠✠✠✠✠✠✠✠✠✠✠✠✠✠✠✠✠✠✠✠✠✠✠✠✠✠

L O N D O N

PRINTED for and SOLD by the BOOKSELLERS.

M DCC LIII.

TO THE

QUEEN.

MADAM,

THE great Honour Your Majefty has done me, in giving me Leave to prefix Your Royal Name to the following Poems, does not encourage me to prefume they are worthy to

be

be laid at Your Feet on any other Account, but only as they are an humble Tribute of Duty, offer'd from a thankful Heart to a gracious Benefactrefs. Your Majefty has indeed the fame Right to them, as You have to the Fruits of a Tree, which You have tranfplanted out of a barren Soil into a fertile and beautiful Garden. It was Your Generofity which brought me out of Obfcurity, and ftill condefcends to protect me; like the Supreme Being, who continually fupports the meaneft Creature, which his Goodnefs has produc'd.

I have Room here to expatiate upon a very inviting Subject; but Your Majefty has nobly prevented

all

all Panegyric, even from the beſt
Pens, by building Your *Fame* on
a much more laſting Baſis, than
that of *Praiſe* in *Dedications.*
Your Encouragements of *Arts* and
Sciences, Your Eſteem and Friend-
ſhip for all Defenders of Truth,
while they are living, the Regard
You pay to their Memories when
dead, and Your generous Care of
their Widows and Orphans, record
Your Virtues in ſuch Characters as
will ever be legible. Your Chriſtian Love to Mankind, Your zealous Endeavours to promote *Reli-*
gion, a Soul made tender to feel
our Misfortunes, and a Will inclin'd to redreſs them, are ſuch
amiable and heavenly Qualities,
as ſhine beſt by their own Light,

A 3 and

and can receive no Luftre from the fineft Defcription.

May Heaven long preferve Your Majefty to practife all thefe Virtues, to be a perpetual Source of Comfort and Joy to our glorious Monarch, a Bleffing to the Nation, and a noble Pattern of Beneficence and Generofity to future Queens. Your Majefty's Great Goodnefs to myfelf draws this Prayer from a Heart fill'd with Gratitude. As. there is fo little Merit in what You now honour with Your Royal Protection, I fhall endeavour to fupply the Defects, the only Way that is in my Power by my Thanks, and Prayers for Your Majefty : *Thefe* I will ever continue, and always make

make it my greateſt Ambition to
ſhew with what profound Reſpect
I am,

MADAM,

Your MAJESTY's.

Moſt Grateful,

Moſt Devoted, and

Moſt Dutiful Servant,

STEPHEN DUCK.

SOME ACCOUNT OF THE LIFE and WRITINGS OF Mr. *STEPHEN DUCK.*

In a LETTER to a FRIEND.

M Y Friend STEPHEN had originally no other Teaching, than what enabled him to read, and write *Englifh* ; he had never taken a fingle Step toward any other Language. As Arithmetic is generally join'd with this Degree of Learning, he had a little Share of that too. About his Fourteenth Year he

he was taken from School, and was afterwards
fuccefïively engag'd in the feveral lowest Em-
ployments of a Country Life. This lasted
for fome Years; fo long, that he had forgot
almost all the Arithmetic he had learn'd at
School: However he read fometimes, and
thought oftner. He had a certain Longing after Knowledge: and when he reflected within
himfelf on his Want of Education, he began
to be particularly uneafy, that he fhould have
forgot fomething of what he had learn'd, even
at the little School he had been at. He thought
of this fo often, that at last he refolv'd to try
his own Strength, and, if poffible, to recover
his Arithmetic again.

His first Attempt of this Kind I take to
have been in the Year 1726. Confidering
the Difficulties the poor Fellow lay under, this
Inclination for Knowledge must have been very
strong in him. He was then married, and at
Service; he had little Time to fpare; he had
no Books, and no Money to get any: But
he was refolv'd to go through with it; and
accordingly us'd to work more than other
Day-labourers, and by that Means got fome
little Matter added to his Pay. This Over-
plus was at his own Difpofal. With this he
bought first a Book of Vulgar Arithmetic, then
one

one of Decimal, and a third of Meafuring of
Land; all which by Degrees he made himfelf
a tolerable Mafter of, in thofe Hours he could
fteal from his Sleep, after the Labours of the
Day.

Where there was fuch a Defire for Knowledge, there muft be good Senfe at bottom, and
a Soul, at leaft, fomewhat above the common
Converfation he muft meet with in his poor
State of Life. I have afk'd him, whom he had
that he could talk and converfe with in the
Country; and was pleas'd to find him, in this
Particular, happier than I expected. He faid,
he had one dear Friend, that he mention'd with
uncommon Affection. They us'd to talk and
read together, when they could fteal a little
Time for it. This Friend had been in a Service
at *London* for two or three Years: He had an
Inclination to Books; he had purchas'd fome,
and brought 'em down with him into the Country; and *Stephen* had always the Ufe of his little Library; which by this Time, poffibly, may
be increas'd to two or three dozen of Books.
This Friend knew no more out of *Englifh* than
Stephen, but by talking together they mutually
improv'd each other. *Stephen* is all Simplicity:
He fays, " That his Friend can talk better
" than he, as having been us'd to more Com-
" pany;

" pany; but that he himſelf has been more
" us'd to Poetry, and in that can do better than
" his Friend.

Had it not been for this, *Stephen* muſt have
been plac'd in the ſame Claſs with *Hai Ebn
Yokdhan*, and the young *Hermes* in Mr. *Ram-
ſay*'s *Cyrus*: But the Story of their Improvements without any Aſſiſtance agrees only with
Romances; and you know, what I am writing
to you is a true Hiſtory. Our retir'd Philoſo-
pher had his Friend; and it ſeems to have
been the greateſt Happineſs of his Life that he
had one. They did not only read, but reaſon'd
over Points together; and I have ſometimes
thought, how agreeable a Thing it would have
been, to have been conceal'd within hearing of
them, when they were in the midſt of ſome of
their moſt knotty Debates. We may imagine
'em both to have had good natural Senſe, and
a few good Books in common between 'em:
Their Minds were their own; neither improv'd,
nor ſpoil'd, by laying in a Stock of Learning:
They were perhaps equally well inclin'd to
learn, both ſtruggling for a little Knowledge;
and, like a Couple of Rowers on the ſame Bottom, while they were only ſtriving perhaps,
which ſhould outdo his Companion, they were
really each helping the other, and driving the
Boat on the faſter. Per-

Perhaps you would be willing to know what Books their little Library confifted of. I need not mention thofe of Arithmetic again, nor his Bible : *Milton*, the *Spectators*, and *Seneca*, were his firft Favourites ; *Telemachus*, with another Piece by the fame Hand, and *Addifon's* Defence of Chriftianity, his next. They had an *Englifh* Dictionary, and a Sort of *Englifh* Grammar, an *Ovid* of long ftanding with them, and a *Byfhe's* Art of Poetry of later Acquifition : *Seneca's* Morals made the Name of *l'Eftrange* dear to them ; and, as I imagine, might occafion their getting his *Jofephus* in Folio, which was the largeft Purchace in their Collection. They had one Volume of *Shakefpeare*, with Seven of his Plays in it. Befide thefe, *Stephen* had read three or four other Plays ; fome of *Epictetus*, *Waller*, *Dryden's Virgil*, *Prior*, *Hudibras*, *Tom Brown*, and the *London Spy*. You may fee I am a faithful Hiftorian, by my giving you the Bad with the Good.

With thefe Helps *Stephen* is grown fomething of a Poet, and fomething of a Philofopher. I find by him, that from his Infancy, he has had a caft in his Mind toward Poetry. He has delighted, as far back as he can remember, in Verfes, and in Singing. He fpeaks of ftrange Emotions that he has felt on the top Performances

B mances

mances of the little Choir of Songsters in a
Country Chancel; and mentions his first hearing
of an Organ, as a remarkable Epocha of his Life.
He seems to be a pretty good Judge too of a
musical Line; but I imagine, that he does not
hear Verses in his own Mind, as he repeats
them. I don't know whether you understand
me. I mean, that his Ideas of Notes in a Verse,
and his Manner of repeating the same Verse,
are often different. For he points out an harmonious Line well enough; and yet he generally spoils its Harmony by his Way of speaking it.

What first gave him a higher Taste of Poetry, than he had been us'd to, was *Milton's*
Paradise Lost. This came oddly enough into
his Hands; and when I see you, I'll tell you
the History of it. *Stephen* read it over twice
or thrice with a Dictionary, before he could
understand the Language of it thoroughly.
This, and a Sort of *English* Grammar they
had, have been of the greatest Use to him of
any Thing.

Indeed it seems plain to me, that he has got
English just as we get *Latin*. He study'd *Pa-*
radise Lost, as others study the Classics. The
new Beauties in that Poem, that were continually

 rily opening upon his Mind, made his Labour eafy to him.   He work'd all Day for his Mafter; and, after the Labour of the Day, fet to his Books at Night.   The Pains he has taken for the Pleafure of improving himfelf are incredible ; but it has anfwer'd too beyond what one could have expected; for he feems to underftand fome of the great and deeper Beauties of that Poem toleiably well , and points out feveral particular Beauties in it, which it requires a good nice Eye to difcover.

'Twas his Friend that help'd him to the *Spectators*; they read them often together, and often by themfelves.   *Stephen* tells me, that he has frequently carry'd them with him to his Work.   When he did fo, his Method was to labour harder than ony body elfe, that he might get Half an Hour to read a *Spectator*, without injuring his Mafter.   By this means he us'd to fit down all over Sweat and Heat, without regarding his own Health, and often to the Prejudice of it.   If this affects you, as it has me, I ought not to pafs it over, that you may not lofe the Pleafure of fo ftrong an Inftance of Honefty and Induftry mix'd together.

The:

The *Spectators* improv'd his Underſtanding,
he ſays, more than any Thing. The Copies
of Verſes ſcatter'd in thoſe Pieces, help'd on
his natural Bent that Way ; and made him willing to try, whether he could not do ſomething
like 'em. He ſometimes turn'd his own
Thoughts into Verſe, while he was at Work ;
and at laſt began to venture thoſe Thoughts a
little on Paper. What he did of this Kind, was
very inconſiderable; only ſcatter'd Thoughts,
and generally not above Four or Five Lines on
the ſame Subject; which, as there was nobody
thereabouts that car'd for Verſes, nor any body
that could tell him whether they were good or
bad, he generally flung into the Fire, as ſoon
as he had pleas'd himſelf enough in reading
them.

Whatever Care he took to burn theſe little
Pieces, he found it not ſufficient to conceal them.
The Thing took Air ; and *Stephen*, who had
before the Name of a Scholar among the
Country People, was ſaid now to be able to
write Verſes too. This was mention'd acci-
dentally, about a Year ago, before a young
Gentleman of *Oxford*, who ſent for *Stephen* ;
and after ſome Talk with him, deſired him to
write him a Letter in Verſe. That Letter is
the Epiſtle which ſtands the firſt in his Poems,
                                                    and

and was the firſt whole Copy of Verſes that ever he wrote. This happen'd to fall into the Hands of ſome Clergymen in the Neighbour-hood, who were very well pleas'd with it ; and upon examining him, found the Man had a good deal of Merit. They gave him ſome Preſents, which, as Things ſtood then, were a great Help to him ; and encourag'd him to go on as much as they could.

This made him proceed with more Courage : And, as he had wrote ſome ſcatter'd Verſes on *Poverty*, before this happen'd, he carry'd thoſe Thoughts on, and fill'd it up, as it ſtands at preſent in the printed Collection I ſend you : So that this is his ſecond Copy. I am very careful in ſettling the Chronology of his Poems, that you may ſee how he has gone on Step by Step, if you pleaſe.

The Compoſition which was next in Order, is that on his own *Labours :* That Subject was given him by one of thoſe who firſt encourag'd him ; and after this was finiſh'd, he was em-ploy'd from the ſame Quarter in his *Shunam-mite*. As this exceeded any of the reſt, I think from hence we may date the Æra of his riſing in Character and Circumſtances. Upon this it was that Perſons of Diſtinction began to ſend for

B 3. him.

him different Ways. In short, it got him Fame enough to be pretty troublesome to him at first; though it is likely to end in a much happier Settlement of him and his Affairs, than could ever have been dreamt of by him at his first setting out.

When you have read his Poems, and consider the Manner he has been bred up in, I doubt not you will think they have their Merit: But I assure you, they give an imperfect Idea of the Man; and, to know how much he deserves, one should converse with him, and hear on what Reasons he omitted such a Part, and introduc'd another; why he shortens his Stile in this Place, and enlarges in that; whence he has such a Word, and whence such an Idea. I'll give you all I can recollect of this Kind, in relation to what is generally reckon'd the best Thing he has wrote, *The Shunammite.*

In the first Place, I found upon enquiry, that he wrote by a Plan; he thought over all the Parts, as he intended to use them, before he made the Verses. For a Poem of any Length, no doubt 'tis as necessary to do this as it is to have a Draught of a House, before you go to building it; and yet I believe, the common Run of our Poets have generally thought themselves felves above it, or not thought of it at all. Tho' the *Shunammite* was written on a Story given to his Hand, ftill fomething of this Kind was convenient enough ; becaufe, in forming it anew, he did not make ufe of all the Materials before him, and has brought in fome of his own. He thought, the Stretching of the Prophet in fo particular a Manner, muft found ftrange. The Woman introduc'd to tell her Story, is a new Caft of his own ; fo is her doubting, and then confirming herfelf again, by a particular Indu-&tion of all *Elifha*'s Miracles ; fo the bringing an Audience about her, and their Chorus's, when they join together in congratulating her Happinefs ; the laft of which clofes the Poem in a good proper Manner.

Upon being afk'd, Why he introduc'd a Perfon to tell all the Story in the *Shunammite,* and why he could not as well tell it himfelf ; he faid, he had read *Prior*'s *Solomon*; and that, in reading it, *Solomon*'s fpeaking every thing touch'd him particularly. He was then afk'd, fince it was to be fpoken, why he did not rather chufe the Prophet, as the Perfon of the greater Dignity, to fpeak it. He faid to this, That the Woman was to be pity'd ; That there feem'd to be * some Expreſſions of the Woman in the Hiſtory, which, if not omitted, might leſſen our Regard and Compaſſion for her ; That, if the Prophet had related the Thing, he could not have omitted a Word ; but when the Woman did, ſhe might well be allow'd to ſoften her own Caſe ; and to drop, when ſhe was cool, any thing wrong, that ſhe ſaid in the Violence of her Grief and Paſſion. This is rather fuller in Words than he expreſs'd it ; but nothing, I think, is added to his Meaning.

As *Milton* had been his favourite Poet, you wonder why none of his Pieces are in Blank Verſe. I aſk'd him about this too: Upon which he told me, That he had originally written the whole *Shunammite* in Blank Verſe ; That, upon reading it over, he found his Language was not ſublime enough for it ; and that therefore he was forc'd to write it all over again, and turn it into Rhyme.

Upon reading over the Chapter and his Poem together, you will ſee how juſtly he ſhortens

and

---

* Such as theſe :

Ver 16. *And ſhe ſaid ; Nay, my Lord, thou Man of God, do not lye unto thy Handmaid.*

Ver. 28, *Did I deſire a Son of my Lord, Did I not ſay, Do not deceive me ?*

and enlarges fome of the particular Paffages, in
order to adapt them the more to Poetry. Be-
fides fome Things already mention'd, he drops
feveral little Circumftances in it. On the †
other hand, he enlarges on the (1) Contented-
nefs and Charities of the Woman ; on the (2)
Look and Attitude of the Prophet ; on her (3)
Thanks for her bearing a Son ; on (4) the Death
of the Child ; on the (5) Reafons of her Confi-
dence in the Prophet ; on (6) pointing out the
Prophet, when fhe comes to him ; and in
his Anfwer ; in her (7) preffing the Prophet
more earneftly to affift her ; in (9) pointing out
the dead Child ; his being (10) freed from
Death ; and her Thoughts (11) upon receiving
him again into her Arms.

'Tis agreeable to fee what Ufe he has made
of the little Reading he can have had, and how
he has improv'd the Thing, by obferving fome
good Strokes in the Books he has met with.
Upon my telling him, that I lik'd nothing better in it, than his altering * the Prophet's Countenance

---

† See 2 Kings, Chap. iv. Verfes 10, 12, 14, 25, 26,
27, 28, 29, 34, and 35.
 (1) Line 33 to 49. (2) 55, &c. (3) 76. (4) 112
to 134 (5) 152, &c. See 205. (6) 211.
 (7) Line 232. (9) 246. (10) 258. (11) 266.
 * From Line 55 to 63.

tenance as he does ; he faid, he took that Hint from *Telemachus* ; where the young Prince comes to *Idomeneus*'s Court, while they are facrificing. The Prieft, on feeing *Telemachus*, breaks off from what he was about, affumes a more infpir'd Air, and begins fpeaking of his future Fortunes. This Alteration of the Prophet's Countenance, *Stephen* fays, he took from thence ; but that at the fame Time he thought himfelf oblig'd to drop the Wildnefs and Enthufiafm of it, in order to adapt it more to the Nature of a true Prophet.

The Chorus in the Clofe of the *Shunammite*, he faid, was brought into his Mind by the † general Rejoicings of the Angels in *Milton*, upon God's finifhing the Creation of the World. The firft Chorus was not in the Work originally ; he inferted it, when he new-form'd it all into Rhyme.

He had alfo been very careful as to fingle Words ; and had Authorities to produce in feveral little Particulars, where one would not expect it. For (1) *flowry Carmel*, he quotes Mr. *Pope* ; and the Prophet's Arbour on the Top of that Mount is cover'd with (2) *Vines*,

on

---

† *Paradife Loft*, Book 7, Line 565, and 602.
(1) The *Shunammite*, Ver. 210. (2) 212.

on the Authority of Mr. *Sandys* in his Travels; For the Words (3) *aduſt* and *ſupernal*, he refers to *Milton*. (4) *Fanatic* he uſes according to the true, and not the Vulgar Senſe of the Word; he had learn'd the proper Meaning of it from the Dictionary: (5) *Dilated Heart*, as ſpoken of Sorrow, is certainly a Fault, but it is a Fault that *Stephen* was naturally enough led into by the common Notions and Expreſſions in the Country, of the Heart's *ſwelling* and being ready to *burſt* with Grief.

He owns his Faults very readily; and if he thinks a Line of his better than ordinary, he will ſay ſo without any Reſerve. He ſeems to be exceedingly open and honeſt in every Thing he ſays. and 'twould be very difficult for you to be with him a Week, as I have been, without going away very much his Friend.

Though I have been ſo long in ſhewing you how critically he has proceeded as to his own Works; I ſhall add ſome of his Thoughts on the Works of others, to give you as full an Idea of him as I can.

'Tis

(3) 117, and 249. (4) 56.
(5) The *Shunammite*, Ver. 143.

'Tis not yet three Years ago that he firſt met with *Milton*; and I believe, that was the firſt Poet of real Value, that he ever ſtudy'd in earneſt. He has aſſur'd me, with all his Innocence and Simplicity, that when he came afterwards to read *Addiſon*'s Criticiſms on *Milton* in the *Spectators*, 'twas a high Pleaſure to him to find many Things mention'd there, in the Praiſe of *Milton*, exactly as he had before thought in reading him. Here we muſt depend on his Credit, which I need not tell you with me is very good.

The Name of *Milton*, whom he admires and dotes on ſo particularly, has not prevail'd on him enough to make him like his *Paradiſe Regain'd*. In ſpeaking of theſe two Poems, he ſaid, " he wonder'd how *Milton* could write ſo incomparably well, where he had ſo little to " lead him; and ſo very poorly, where he had " more.

The *Spectators*, you know, he has read with great Pleaſure, and great Improvement. I remember particularly, that on ſomebody's calling them *Proſe*, he ſaid, " 'Twas true, they " were *Proſe*; but there was ſomething in 'em " that pleas'd almoſt like *Verſe*."----He mention'd, with more Regard than uſual, the critical

Paper

Papers on wit, thofe on *Milton*, the *Juſtum &
tenacem* from *Horace*, Mr. *Pope's Meſſiah*, and
the feveral fcatter'd ones written in the Caufe
of Virtue and Religion.

Upon afking him what Plays he had read,
he nam'd particularly *Julius Cæſar*, *Hamlet*,
Cato, *Venice Preſerv'd*, and the *Orphan*. *Venice
Preſerv'd*, he faid, gave him the moſt *Horror* ;
a Word which I took Notice he us'd fometimes
for Sorrow, and fometimes in its proper Senfe :
He could not bear the comic Parts in it. *Hamlet* he lik'd better than *Julius Cæſar* ; and in
Hamlet pointed out that celebrated Speech, *To
be, or not to be*, &c. as having been his favour-
rite Part, merely of his own Taſte He did
not admire *Shakeſpear's* Comedy ; and faid,
" He was too high, and too low." I read
over to him fome of *Hamlet*, and the celebrated
Speeches of *Antony* to the People in *Julius Cæſar*. He trembled, as I read the Ghoſt's Speech ;
and admir'd the Speeches and Turns in the Mob
round *Cæſar's* Body, more he faid, than ever
he had done before. As I was reading to him,
I obſerv'd that his Countenance chang'd often
in the moſt moving Parts : His Eye was quick
and bufy all the Time ; and, to fay the Truth,
I never faw Applaufe, or the fhifting of proper
Paſſions, appear fo ſtrongly in any Face as in
his.   C   He

He had formerly read *Tom Brown's Letters from the Dead*, and the *London Spy*, not without some Pleasure; but, after he had been some Time conversant with the *Spectators*, he said, " He did not care much to look into them " He spoke of *Hudibras* in another Manner; he saw a great deal of Wit in it, and was particularly pleas'd with the Conjurer's Part in that Poem : But, after all, 'tis not a Manner of Writting that he can so sincerely delight in, as in the Moral, the Passionate, or the Sublime.

Indeed what every body seems to admire him for, is, that he seems to have an excellent moral Turn in his Thoughts. He is, as I told you before, something of a Philosopher; and, what is better than a Philosopher, a good honest-hearted Man. He has read, and speaks highly of, the Archbishop of *Cambray*'s Demonstration of the Being of a God, and Mr. *Addison*'s Defence of the Christian Religion. He said, " That they touch'd his Mind; and " that nothing did so well, as when one's Rea- " son is mov'd by what is said." He had lik'd the little he had read of *Epictetus*, but 'twas *Seneca* that had made him happy in his own Mind. He seems as yet not to be hurt at all by any Applauses that have been given him, and to have been perfectly contented with his Condi-

tion

ton before : When he had only receiv'd fome Prefents from Gentlemen in the Country, he was quite eafy as to his Circumftances. The only Thing then, that he was folicitous about, was, how he might fucceed as to the Poetry he fhould be employ'd in. This was his chief Concern · But even this feem'd to proceed not fo much from any Defire of Fame, as from a Principle of Gratitude, or, as he exprefs'd it, his Longing to pleafe thofe Friends that had been fo generous to him. He was not lifted up with the Character fome People gave him, and talk'd of Fame abfolutely like a Philofopher. After his beft Fortune, many of his Friends told him the Danger of being vain; and, if he fhould once be fo, that he would be as much defpis'd as he had been applauded. He faid, "That "he could not well tell what they meant; That "he did not know what it was to be vain ; But, "fince fo many great Men, who knew the "World fo much better than he did, were ap-"prehenfive for him on that Head, he began "to be terribly alarm'd at his Danger, tho' he "had no fettled Ideas of what it was." He was told upon this, That he fhould never fpeak too highly in Praife of the Poems he had writ-ten. He faid, "If that was all, he was fafe ; "that was a Thing he could never do, for he "could not think highly of them: Gentle-

" men indeed, he faid, might like 'em, becaufe
" they were made by a poor Fellow in a Barn;
" but that he knew, as well as any body, that
" they were not really good in themfelves

Thus, Sir, I have obey'd your Commands
as faithfully as I am able. You defired me not
to fpare Paper; but to fend you a Book rather
than a Letter. You fee I have taken you at
your Word; and that I am refolved in this, as
well as in every thing elfe, to fhew you how
punctually I would ever be,

S   I   R,

Your moft humble Servant

J. SPENCE.

P O E M S

O N

SEVERAL OCCASIONS.

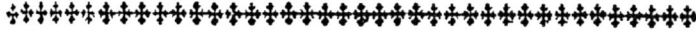

✛✛

To a Gentleman, *who requested a Copy of* Verses
*from the Author ; being the first finish'd Copy
he ever wrote.*

S I R,

I Have, before the Time prescrib'd by you,
Expos'd my weak Production to your
    View;
Which may, I hope, have Pardon at your
    Hand,
Becaufe produc'd to Light by your Command.
Perhaps you might expect fome finish'd Ode,
Or facred Song, to found the Praife of GOD;

C 3   A

A glorious Thought, and laudable ! But then
Think what illit'rate Poet guides the Pen :
Ill suit such Tasks with One who holds the Plough,
Such lofty Subjects to a Fate so low.

    Sir, were your Eloquence and Learning mine,
And I, like you, a Fav'rite of the Nine ,
I quickly would *Parnassus* Summit climb,
And find a Hero worthy of my Rhyme :
Nor should my Muse the *Grecian* Monarchs trace,
Nor would I celebrate the *Trojan* Race;
Nor any of those martial Sons of Fame,
Pagans, unworthy of a Christian's Theme
Far nobler Thoughts my grateful Voice should raise,
In lofty Strains, to great MESSIAH's Praise
I'd joyfully resound his wond'rous Birth,
And paint his Godlike Virtues, whilst on Earth ,
Then, with Reluctance, Horror, and Surprize,
I'd mournfully relate his Agonies ,
I'd trace the heavenly Hero to the Tree,
Sing what he suffer'd there for you and me ;
Next, in heroic Numbers, would I tell,
How soon he baffled Death and vanquish'd Hell,
Subdu'd the Grave, and shew'd the glorious Way,
From Realms of Darkness to eternal Day.
Such nobler Subjects should my Lays excite ,
And you, my Patron, would in such delight;
Grateful to me, when you, well pleas'd, should view
The accomplish'd sacred Song inscrib'd to you.

    But now I must omit MESSIAH's Praise,
Left I degrade him with unworthy Lays,
My Fate compels me silent to remain,
For want of Learning to improve my Strain ·
By which no Thought, tho' well conceiv'd, can rise,
To full Perfection, but in Embryo dies :

                                   Yet

Yet my unpolifh'd Genius will produce,
And bring forth fomething, tho' of little Ufe.

Thus, in the Country, often have I found,
Thro' flothful Man's Neglect, a Plat of Ground,
Wafte and uncultivated, void of Seeds,
Producing Nothing, but fome trifling Weeds.

But why ftand I my Fate accufing fo ?
The Field calls me to Labour; I muft go :
The Kine low after Meat, the hungry Steed,
Neighing, complains he wants his ufual Feed.
Then, Sir, adieu. Accept what you did crave,
And be propitious to your humble Slave.

On POVERTY.

NO Ill on Earth we tim'rous Mortals fly
With fo much Dread as abject Poverty :
O defpicable Name! We, thee to fhun,
On ev'ry other Evil blindly run.
For Fear of thee, diftruftful Nigards go
In tatter'd Rags, and ftarve their Bodies too,
And ftill are poor, for Fear of being fo.
For Fear of thee, the cheating Trader vows,
His Wares are good, altho' his Confcience knows,
He has employ'd his utmoft Skill and Care,
To hide their Faults, and make them Beauties glare.
The Sailor, terrify'd with Thoughts of thee,
Boldly attempts the Dangers of the Sea ,
From Eaft to Weft, o'er Rocks and Quickfands fteers ;
'Tis Poverty, and that alone, he fears ;

The

The Soldier too, whom nought but thee can fcare,
In Hopes of Plunder, bravely meets the War;
To fly from Poverty, he runs on Death,
And fhews he prizes Riches more than Breath,
Strange Terror of Mankind! By thee mifled,
Not Confcience, Quickfands, Rocks, or Death, they
     dread!
And yet thou art no formidable Foe,
Except to little Souls, who think thee fo:
Who thro' the Glafs of Prejudice furvey
Thy Face, a thoufand frightful Forms difplay.

    Thus Men, at Night, in foolifh Fears grown old,
Who mind the fairy Tales their Nurfes told,
Start at a Goblin, which their Fancy made,
And, for a Spectre, often take a Shade.

    Contented Poverty's no difmal Thing,
Free from the Cares unwieldy Riches bring:
At Diftance both alike deceive our View;
Nearer approach'd, they take another Hue
The poor Man's Labour relifhes his Meat;
His Morfel's pleafant, and his Reft is fweet
Not fo the Rich, who find their weary'd Tafte
Pall'd with the Profpect of the cumb'rous Feaft;
For what they have more than they can enjoy,
Inftead of fatisfying, does but cloy.

    But let us ftate the Cafe another Way.
Were Poverty fo hideous as they fay,
'Tis nobler chearfully to bear our Fate,
Than murmur and repine beneath its Weight.
The Man deferves the Praife of human Kind,
Who bears ill Fortune with a Chriftian Mind.
How does his great heroic Soul afpire
Above that fordid Wealth the reft admire!

His

His nobler Thoughts are fix'd on Things above;
His faithful Eyes surveys the God of Love
Hold forth the heavenly Prize, which makes him run
His mortal Race, to gain th'immortal Crown.
Not all the Snares a crafty Dev'l can lay,
Can intercept, or daunt him in his Way.
Not all the scornful Insults of the Proud,
Not all the Censures of the grov'ling Croud,
Not Poverty, in all her Terrors drest,
Can shake the solid quiet of his Breast
Unmov'd he stands against the worst of Foes,
And mocks the Darts, which adverse Fortune throws,
Calm and compos'd, amidst or Ease or Pain,
And finds Content, which others seek in vain.

So stands a steady Rock, sublimely steep,
Within the Confines of the briny Deep,
Lash'd by the foaming Surge on ev'ry Side,
Yet can't be shaken by the furious Tide.

Then why should Phantoms discompose the Mind;
Or Woes, so far from real, fright Mankind?
Since Wealth can never make the Vicious blest,
Nor Poverty subdue the virtuous Breast;
Since both from Heav'n's unerring Hand are sent,
LORD, give me either, give me but CONTENT.

The THRESHER's Labour.

To the Reverend Mr. STANLEY.

THE grateful Tribute of thefe rural-Lays,
 Which to her Patron's Hand the Mufe conveys,
Deign to accept 'Tis juft the Tribute bring
To him, whofe Bounty gives her Life to fing;
To him, whofe gen'rous Favours tune her Voice;
And bid her, 'midft her Poverty, rejoice.
Infpir'd by thefe, fhe dares herfelf prepare,
To fing the Toils of each revolving Year;
Thofe endlefs Toils, which always grow anew,
And the poor *Threfher's* deftin'd to purfue:
Ev'n thefe, with Pleafure, can the Mufe rehearfe,
When you and Gratitude demand her Verfe.

Soon as the golden Harveft quits the Plain,
And CERES' Gift's reward the Farmer's Pain;
What Corn each Sheaf will yield, intent to hear,
And guefs from thence the Profits of the Year,
He calls his Reapers forth : Around we ftand,
With deep Attention, waiting his Command.
To each our Tafk he readily divides,
And pointing, to our diff'rent Stations guides.
As he directs, to diftant Barns we go;
Here two for Wheat, and there for Barley two.
But firft, to fhew what he expects to find,
Thefe Words, or Words like thefe, difclofe his Mind.

" So dry the Corn was carry'd from the Field,
" So eafily 'twill threfh, fo well 'twill yield;
" Sure large Day's-Works I well may hope for now.
" Come, ftrip, and try, let's fee what you can do."

Divefted

Divefted of our Cloaths, with Flail in Hand,
At proper Diftance, Front to Front we ftand.
And firft the Threfhal's gently fwung, to prove,
Wh ther with juft Exactnefs it will move
That once fecure, we fwiftly whirl them round,
From the ftrong Planks our Crab-tree Staves rebound,
And echoing Barns return the ratling Sound.
Now in the Air our knotty Weapons fly,
And now with equal Force defcend from high;
Down one, one up, fo well they keep the Time,
The Cyclops' Hammers could not truer chime;
Nor with more heavy Strokes could *Ætna* groan,
When Vulcan forg'd the Arms for Thetis' Son.
In briny Streams our Sweat defcends apace,
Drops from our Locks, or trickles down our Face.
No Intermiffion in our Work we know,
The noify Threfhal muft for ever go
Their Mafter abfent, others fafely play;
The fleeping Threfhal does itfelf betray.
Nor yet, the tedious Labour to beguile,
And make the paffing Minutes fweetly fmile,
Can we, like Shepherds, tell a merry Tale,
The Voice is loft, drown'd by the louder Flail.
But we may think —— Alas! what pleafing Thing,
Here, to tne Mind, can the dull Fancy bring
Our Eye beholds no pleafing Object here,
No chearful Sound diverts our lift'ning Ear.
The Shepherd well may tune his Voice to fing,
Infpir'd with all the Beauties of the Spring
No Fountains murmur here, no Lambkins play,
No Linnets warble, and no Fields look gay,
'Tis all a gloomy, melancholy Scene,
Fit only to provoke the Mufe's Spleen
When footy Peafe we threfh, you fcarce can know
Our native Colour, as from Work we go:

The

The Sweat, the Duſt, and ſuffocating Smoke,
Make us ſo much like *Ethiopians* look,
We ſcare our Wives, when Ev'ning brings us home,
And frighted Infants think the Bugbear come
Week after Week, we this dull Taſk purſue,
Unleſs when winn wing Days produce a new;
A new, indeed, but frequently a worſe!
The Threſhal yields but to the Maſter's Curſe.
He counts the Buſhels, counts how much a Day;
He ſwears we've idled half our Time away
" Why, look ye, Rogues, d'ye think that this will do"
" Your Neighbours thraſh as much again as you"
Now in our Hands we wiſh our noiſy Tools,
To drown the hated Names of Rogues and Fools.
But wanting theſe, we juſt like School-boys look,
When angry Maſters view the blotted Book
They cry, " their Ink was faulty, and their Pen,"
We, " the Corn threſhes bad, 'twas cut too green."

But ſoon as *Winter* hides his hoary Head,
And Nature's Face is with new Beauty ſpread,
The lovely *Spring* appears, refreſhing Show'rs
New cloath the Field with Graſs, and blooming Flow'rs
Next to her the rip'ning *Summer* preſſes on,
And Sol begins his longeſt Race to run.
Before the Door our welcome Maſter ſtands;
Tells us the ripen'd Graſs requires our Hands.
The grateful Tiding preſently imparts
Life to our Looks, and Spirits to our Hearts.
We wiſh the happy Seaſon may be fair;
And, joyful, long to breathe in op'ner Air.
This Change of Labour ſeems to give ſuch Eaſe,
With Thoughts of Happineſs ourſelves we pleaſe.
But, ah! how rarely's Happineſs complete!
There's always Bitter mingled with the Sweet.
When firſt the Lark ſings Prologue to the Day,
We riſe, admoniſh'd by his early Lay,

This

This new Employ with eager Haste to prove,
This new Employ, becomes so much our Love.
Alas! that human Joys shou'd change so soon!
Our Morning Pleasure turns to Pain at Noon.
The Birds salute us, as to Work we go,
And with new Life our Bosoms seem to glow.
On our right Shoulder hangs the crooked Blade,
The Weapon destin'd to uncloath the Mead;
Our left supports the Whetstone, Scrip, and Beer;
This for our Scythes, and these ourselves to chear.
And now the Field, design'd to try our Might,
At length appears, and meets our longing Sight.
The Grass and Ground we view with careful Eyes,
To see which Way the best Advantage lies,
And, Hero like, each claims the foremost Place.
At first our Labour seems a sportive Race
With rapid Force our sharpen'd Blades we drive,
Strain every Nerve, and Blow for Blow we give.
All strive to vanquish, tho' the Victor gains,
No other Glory, but the greatest Pains.

But when the scorching Sun is mounted high,
And no kind Barns with friendly Shade are nigh,
Our weary Scythes entangle in the Grass,
While Streams of Sweat run trickling down apace.
Our sportive Labour we too late lament;
And with that Strength again we vainly spent.

Thus, in the Morn, a Courser have I seen
With headlong Fury scour the level Green;
Or mount the hills, if Hills are in his Way,
As if no Labour could his Fire allay,
Till PHOEBUS, shining with meridian Heat,
Has bath'd his panting Sides in briny Sweat:
The lengthen'd Chace scarce able to sustain,
He measures back the Hills and Dales with Pain.

D   With

With Heat and Labour tir'd, our Scythes we quit,
Search out a shady Tree and down we sit:
From Scrip and Bottle hope new Strength to gain;
But Scrip and Bottle too are try'd in vain.
Down our parch'd Throats we scarce the Bread can get,
And, quite o'erspent with Toil, but faintly eat,
Nor can the Bottle only answer all,
The Bottle and the Beer are both too small.
Time flows. Again we rise from off the Grass;
Again each Mower takes his proper Place,
Not eager now, as late, our Strength to prove;
But all contented regular to move.
We often whet, and often view the Sun;
As often wish, his tedious Race was run.
At length he veils his purple Face from Sight,
And bids the weary Labourer, Good Night.
Homewards we move, but spent so much with Toil,
We slowly walk, and rest at ev'ry Stile
Our good expecting Wives, who think we stay,
Got to the Door, soon eye us in the Way.
Then from the Pot the Dumplin's catch'd in Haste,
And homely by its Side the Bacon plac'd.
Supper and Sleep by Morn new Strength supply;
And out we set again, our Work to try;
But not so early quite, nor quite so fast,
As, to our Cost, we did the Morning past.

Soon as the rising Sun has drank the Dew,
Another Scene is open to our View
Our Master comes, and at his Heels a Throng
Of prattling Females, arm'd with Rake and Prong;
Prepar'd, whilst he is here, to make his Hay,
Or, if he turns his Back, prepar'd to play;
But here, or gone, sure of this Comfort still;
Here's Company, so they may chat their Fill.
Ah! were their Hands so active as their Tongues,
How nimbly then would move the Rakes and Prongs
The

The Grass again is spread upon the Ground,
Till not a vacant Place is to be found,
And while the parching Sun-beams on it shine,
The Hay-makers have Time allow'd to dine.
That soon dispatch'd, they still sit on the Ground,
And the brisk Chat renew'd, afresh goes round.
All talk at once, but seeming all to fear,
That what they speak, the rest will hardly hear;
Till by degrees so high their Notes they strain,
A Stander-by can nought distinguish plain.
So loud's their Speech, and so confus'd their Noise,
Scarce puzzled Echo can return the Voice.
Yet, spite of this, they bravely all go on,
Each scorns to be, or seem to be outdone.
Mean-while the changing Sky begins to lour,
And hollow Winds proclaim a sudden Show'r;
The tattling Croud can scarce their Garments gain,
Before descends the thick impetuous Rain,
Their noisy Prattle all at once is done,
And to the Hedge they soon for Shelter run.

Thus have I seen, on a bright Summer's Day,
On some green Brake, a Flock of Sparrows play;
From Twig to Twig, from Bush to Bush they fly,
And with continued Chirping fill the Sky.
But, on a sudden, if a Storm appears,
Their chirping Noise no longer dins our Ears,
They fly for Shelter to the thickest bush;
There silent sit, and all at once is hush.

But better Fate succeeds the rainy Day,
And little Labour serves to make the Hay.
Fast as 'tis cut, so kindly shines the Sun,
Turn'd once or twice, the pleasing work is done
Next Day the Cocks appear in equal Rows,
Which the glad Master in safe Ricks bestows.

The

The spacious Fields we now no longer range,
And yet, hard Fate! still Work for Work we change,
Back to the Barns we hastily are sent,
Where lately so much Time we pensive spent:
Not pensive now, we bless the friendly Shade,
And to avoid the parching Sun are glad.
Yet little Time we in the Shade remain,
Before our Master calls us forth again;
And says, " For Harvest now yourselves prepare,
" The ripen'd Harvest now demands your Care.
" Get all Things ready, and be quickly drest,
" Early next Morn I shall disturb your Rest."
Strict to his Word! for scarce the Dawn appears,
Before his hasty Summons fills our Ears.
His hasty Summons we obey, and rise,
While yet the Stars are glimm'ring in the Skies.
With him our Guide we to the Wheat-field go,
He to appoint, and we the Work to do.

Ye Reapers, cast your Eyes around the Field,
And view the various Scenes its Beauties yield
Then look again, with a more tender Eye,
To think how soon it must in Ruin lie!
For, once set in, where-e'er our Blows we deal,
There's no resisting of the well-whet Steel
But here or there, where'ere our Course we bend,
Sure Desolation does our Steps attend

Thus, when, *Arabia's* Sons, in Hopes of Prey,
To some more fertile Country take their Way,
How beauteous all Things in the Morn appear!
There rural Cots, and pleasant Villa's here!
So many grateful Objects meet the Sight,
The ravish'd Eye could willing gaze till Night.
But long 'ere then, where-e'er their Troops have past,
These pleasing Prospects lie a gloomy Waste.

The

The Morning past, we sweat beneath the Sun;
And but uneasily our Work goes on.
Before us we perplexing Thistles find,
And Corn blown adverse with the ruffling Wind.
Behind our Master waits, and if he spies
One charitable Ear, he grudging cries,
" Ye scatter half your Wages o'er the Land "
Then scrapes the Stubble with his greedy Hand.

Let those who feast at Ease on dainty Fare.
Pity the Reapers, who their Feasts prepare.
For Toils scarce ever ceasing press us now;
Rest never does, but on the Sabbath, show;
And barely that our Masters will allow.
Think what a painful Life we daily lead;
Each Morning early rise, go late to Bed;
Nor, when asleep, are we secure from Pain;
We then perform our Labours o'er again.
Our mimic Fancy ever restless seems;
And what we act awake, she acts in Dreams.
Hard Fate ! our Labours ev'n in Sleep don't cease ;
Scarce HERCULES e'er felt such Toils as these !

But soon we rise the bearded Crop again,
Soon PHOEBUS' Rays well dry the golden Grain.
Pleas'd with the Scene, our Master glows with Joy ;
Bids us for carrying all our Force employ ;
When straight Confusion o'er the Field appears,
And stunning Clamour fill the Workmen's Ears ;
The Bells and clashing Whips alternate sound,
And rattling Waggons thunder o'er the Ground.
The Wheat, when carry'd, Pease, and other Grain,
We soon secure, and leave a fruitless Plain ;
In noisy Triumph the last Load moves on,
And loud Huzza's proclaim the Harvest done.

Our

Our Master, joyful at the pleasing Sight,
Invites us all to feast with him at Night.
A Table plentifully spread we find,
And jugs of huming Ale to chear the Mind ;
Which he, 'too gen'rous, pushes round so fast,
We think no Toils to come, nor mind the past.
But the next Morning soon reveals the Cheat,
When the same Toils we must again repeat,
To the same Barns must back again return,
To labour there for Room for next Year's Corn.

Thus, as the Year's revolving Course goes round,
No Respite from our Labour can be found
Like Sisyphus, our Work is never done,
Continually rolls back the restless Stone
New-growing Labours still succeed the past;
And growing always new, must always last

The S H U N A M M I T E.

To Mrs. S T A N L E Y.

DEIGN, heav'nly Muses, to assist my Song·
To heav'nly Muses heav'nly Themes belong.
But chiefly Thou, O GOD, my Soul inspire,
And touch my Lips with thy celestial Fire.
If Thou delight'st in flow'ry Carmel's Shade,
Or Jordan's Stream ; from thence I crave thy Aid.

Instruct

Instruct my Tongue, and my low Accents raise,
To sing thy Wonders, and display thy Praise:
Thy Praise let all the Sons of *Judah* hear,
And to my Song the distant Tribes repair.

So pray'd the *Shunammite*, Heav'n heard the Dame;
The distant Tribes around her list'ning came,
To hear th'amazing Tale, while thus her Tongue,
Mov'd by some heav'nly Pow'r, began the Song.

Attend, ye Seed of ABRAM, and give Ear,
While I JEHOVAH's glorious Acts declare
How Life from Death, and Joy from Sadness spring,
If he assist the Muse, the Muse shall sing.
My Lord and I, to whom all bounteous Heav'n
His Blessings with no sparing Hand had giv'n,
Like faithful Stewards of our wealthy Store,
Still lodg'd the Stranger and reliev'd the Poor.
And as ELISHA, by divine Command,
Came preaching Virtue to a sinful Land,
He often deign'd to lodge within our Gate,
And oft receiv'd an hospitable Treat
A decent Chamber for him we prepar'd;
And He, the gen'rous Labour to reward,
Honours in Camp, or Court, to us propos'd;
Which I refus'd, and thus my Mind disclos'd,

Heav'n's King has plac'd us in a fertile Land,
Where he show'rs down his Gifts with copious Hand:
Already we enjoy a fluent Store;
Why should we be solicitous for more?
Give martial Camps and kingly Courts to them,
Who place their only Bliss in fleeting Fame.
There let them live in golden Chains of State;
And be unhappy only to be great.

But

But let us in our native Soil remain,
Nor barter Happiness for fordid Gain.
Here may we feed the Indigent in Peace,
Or cloath the Bare with the fuperfluous Fleece,
And give the weary fainting Pilgrim' Eafe
This we prefer to Pomp and formal Show.
Which only ferve to varnish o'er our Woe,
Refulgent Ornaments, which drefs the Proud,
Objects of Wonder to the gazing Croud;
Yet feldom give Content, or folid Reft,
To the vain Man by whom they are poffefs'd.

All Bleffings but a Child, had Heav'n fupply'd;
And only that th'Almighty had deny'd
Which when the holy prefcient Sage had heard,
He faid, and I before him ftraight appear'd,
And, as my Feet approach'd his awful Room,
I faw his Face diviner Looks affume.
Not fuch a Wildnefs, and fanatic Mien,
With which, fome fay, the *Delphic* Priefts are feen;
When they, for Myfteries of Fate, explain
The odd Chimera's of a frantic Brain,
But with a grave majeftic Air he ftood,
While more than Human in his Afpect glow'd.
Celeftial Grace fat on his radiant Look,
And Pow'r diffufive fhone before he fpoke.
Then thus " Hail gen'rous Soul! thy pious Cares
" Are not forgot, nor fruitlefs are thy Prayers
" Propitious Heav'n, thy virtuous Deeds to crown,
" Shall make thy barren Womb conceive a Son."
So fpake the Seer, and, to compleat my Joy,
As he had fpoke, I bore the promis'd Boy.

Soon to my Friends the welcome News was known,
Who crouded in apace to fee my Son.
Hailing, with kind Salutes, the recent Child;
And, with their pious Hymns, my Pain beguil'd.
When

When all had said, I mov'd my joyful Tongue;
And thus to Heav'n address'd my grateful Song

" O God, what Eloquence can sing thy Praise?
' Or who can fathom thy stupendous Ways?
' All Things obey at thy divine Command,
' Thou mak'st a fruitful Field of barren Land:
' Obdurate Rocks a fertile Glebe shall be,
' And bring forth copious Crops, if bid by Thee;
' *Arabian* Deserts shall with Plenty smile,
' And curling Vines adorn the sterile Soil '

As thus she spake her Audience raise their Voice;
And interrupt her Song as they rejoice
' O God, we gladly hear thy mighty Pow'r,
' With joyful Heart thy gracious Name adore:
' All Nature is subservient to thy Word,
' And shifts her wonted Course, to please her Lord
' We for thy Servant's Joy, our Thanks express,
' As grows the Child, so may her Bliss increase:
' And may the Guardian Angels, who preside
' Over the Bless'd, his future Actions guide;
' Make spotless Virtue crown his vital Date,
' And hoary Honour end his Life but late;
' Then safely bear"—The Dame here wav'd her Hand;
The People straight obey her mute Command
All silent stand, and all attentive look,
Waiting her Words, while thus she mournful spoke:

All Pleasur's are imperfect here below;
Our sweetest Joys are mix'd with bitter Woe·
The Draught of Bliss, when in our Goblet cast,
Is dash'd with Grief, or spilt before we taste.
Ere twice four Years were measur'd by my Son,
(So soon, alas! the greatest Blessing's gone)
In Harvest time he to the Reapers goes,
To view the bearded Sheaves, erect in Rows,

Like

Like an embattled Army in the Field ;
A new delightful Prospect to the Child !
But either there the scorching Sun display'd
His Heat intense, and on his Vitals prey'd ;
Or else some sudden apoplectic Pain,
With racking Torture seiz'd his tender Brain;
His Spirits fail'd, he straight began to faint,
And to his Father vainly made Complaint
The glowing Rose was quickly seen to fade
At once his Beauty, and his Life decay'd.

Soon, at my House, the dismal News I heard,
Soon at my House the dying Child appear'd
T'embrace him I, with fond Affection, run ,
And, Oh ! said I, what Pain afflicts my Son ?
He try'd to speak , but, fault'ring gave a Groan,
No perfect Word proceeded from his Tongue,
But on his Lips the broken Accents hung.
All Means I us'd, that might allay his Pain ,
All Means I us'd, but us'd them all in vain
Yet, while he liv'd, my Soul would not despair,
Nor, till he ceas'd to breathe, I ceas'd my Pray'r.
Deluding Hope now stopt the falling Tears ,
Now his increasing Pains increas'd my Fears
By Hope and Fear alternate was I tost,
Till Hope, in a sad Certainty was lost.
Short, and more short, he drew his panting Breath
(Too sure Presage of his approaching Death !)
Till soon the Blood, congealing, ceas'd to flow ,
He dropt his Head, with a declining Bow
Thrice, from my Breast, to raise himself he try'd,
And thrice sunk down again , then, groaning dy'd.

Thus, when with Care we've nurs'd a tender Vine
And taught the docile Branches where to twine ,
An Eastern Gale, or some pernicious Frost,
Nips the young Tree, and all our Labour's lost.
                                                    Wit

With Horror chill'd, a while I speechless stood,
Viewing the Child, and trembling as I view'd:
My Eyes discharg'd their humid Store apace,
And Tears succeeded Tears adown my Face:
Scarcely my Heart the Load of Grief sustain'd;
At length, recov'ring Speech, I thus complain'd:

O fleeting Joys, inconstant as the Wind!
Which only for a Moment please the Mind,
Then fly, and leave a Weight of Woes behind!
But yet in vain I thus lament and mourn;
The Soul, once fled, shall never more return;
And the fair Body now must be convey'd
To Earth's dark Bosom, and eternal Shade——
Yet let me not prescribe a Bound to Heav'n;
I was by a Miracle the Child was giv'n,
Nor can I think the Wonder is more great,
Should the departed Soul resume her Seat.
What if I to Mount *Carmel* haste away,
To him who did his mystic Birth display?
His pow'rful Word the Barren fruitful made;
His pow'rful Word, perhaps, may raise the Dead.
The famous *Tishbite* rais'd a Widow's Son,
ELISHA has as wond'rous Actions done
When he to *Jordan*'s rapid Torrent came;
And, with the Mantle, smote th'impetuous Stream;
Obsequious to the Stroke, the Waves divide;
And raise a liquid Wall on either Side!
At *Jericho* long had the barren Soil
Deceiv'd the Husbandman, and mock'd his Toil;
Yet, at his Word, it grew a fertile Field,
And pois'nous Springs did wholesome Waters yield.
Nor can he only such great Blessings send,
But Curses, if invok'd, his Call attend
Else how at *Bethel* brought he Vengeance down,
As a just Scourge, on that approbrious Town?

Again

Again, when *Moab* Peace with *Israel* broke;
And vainly strove to quit the fertile Yoke,
Our pow'rful Kings led forth th' embattled Host
Thro' *Edom*'s fultry Wilds, and Air aduft.
Where the confed'rate Troops no Water found,
Dry were the Springs, and sterile was the Ground;
The Captains wanted Strength and Courage fail'd,
When Thirst and Foes at once their Host affail'd
The Kings to h r their joint Petitions made,
And fainting Soldiers crav'd his timely Aid,
Nor crav'd in vain, The pow'ful Word he spake
And flowing Waters form'd a spacious Lake,
The fhining Streams advanc'd their humid Train,
'Till *Faom*'s Wilds became a liquid Plain.
Not in more Plenty did the Waters run
Out of the Rock, when ftruck by AMRAM's Son.
And who can that amazing Deed forget,
Which he perform'd to pay the Widow's Debt?
Whofe Quantity of Oil one Pot contain'd,
Yet num'rous Veffels fill'd, before 'twas drain'd.
Sure he, who fuch ftupendous Acts has done,
If GOD propitious prove, can raife my Son.

So faying, up I caught the Child with Speed;
And laid him on the facred Prophet's Bed,
Then call'd my Servant to prepare the Steed.
Penfive and fad, my mourning Hufband faid,
'Tis now in vain to crave ELISHA's Aid,
No God To day the Prophet does infpire;
Nor can he anfwer what thou wouldft inquire.

Rather than fink, faid I, attempt to raife
My Hopes, nor talk of ceremonial Days,
His God is prefent ftill, and hears him when he prays.
Thus faid, urging my Steed with eager Hafte,
Swift as a Mountain Roe, the Plains I pafs'd,

O'r

O'er Hills and Dales my Journey I pursu'd;
Nor slack'd my Pace, till *Carmel's* mount I view'd;
On whose delightful Brow, in cool Retreat,
Among the curling Vines the Prophet sat;
Whose twining Arms a verdant Arbour made;
The verdant Arbour form'd a grateful Shade.
The fanning Zephyrs gently play'd around,
And shook the trembling Leaves, and swept the Ground.
Down humbly at his Feet I prostrate fell,
Submiss, and, weeping, told the mournful Tale.

Strive to compose thy anxious Soul, said he;
Tears can't revoke JEHOVAH's fix'd Decree:
We live and die, and both, as he thinks fit,
Who may command but Mortals must submit.
This Fate the King, as well as Peasant, finds,
Nor is it evil, but to evil Minds ———
Yet if from Heav'n I can my Suit obtain,
Thy lifeless Son shall yet revive again.

Thus said, with Looks divine, his Staff he views,
As if some pow'rful Charm he would infuse.
Then calls his Servant hastily, and said,
On the Child's Face let this be quickly laid.

O Thou, said I, on whom my Hopes depend,
Do not this Work to Servants Care commend:
If Thou thyself with me refuse to go,
Here, to the list'ning Vines, I'll vent My Woe;
Still prostrate lie, lamenting for my Son,
Till ev'ry Hill prove vocal to my Moan
More had I said, but Grief the Words suppreft;
Yet Sighs, and silent Tears explain'd the rest.
At length he from his verdant Seat arose,
And hastily adown the Mountain goes ·
To *Shunem* we, with Speed, our Way pursue;
The City soon appears within our View,

b An

And the obedient Servant at the Gate,
Returning fad, without Succefs, we met ·
The beauteous Child by Death ftill vanquifh'd lay;
Still Death infulted o'er the beauteous Prey:
Till to the Houfe the facred Seer was come,
And, with fupernal Pow'r, approach'd the Room.

By the dead Child, a while he penfive ftood,
Then from the Chamber put the mourning Crowd,
That done, to God he made his ardent Pray'r,
And breath'd upon the Child with vital Air;
And now the Soul refumes her priftine Seat,
And now the Heart again begins to beat,
Life's purple Current o'er the Body fpreads,
While Death, repuls'd, inglorioufly recedes.

Thus, when a prowling Wolf has ftol'n a Lamb,
He fternly guards it from the bleating Dam,
But if the Keeper comes, he quits his Prey,
And low'ring, with Reluctance, makes away.

And now the Prophet, to my longing Arms,
Refign'd the Child, with more than wonted Charms:
The blufhing Rofe fhone frefher in his Face,
And Beauty fmil'd with a fuperior Grace.

So, when Heav'n's Lamp, that rules the genial Day,
Behind the fable Moon purfues his Way,
Affrighted Mortals, when th'Eclipfe is o'er,
Believe him more illuftrious than before.

Here ends the Dame, and the promifcuous Throng,
With Hallelujahs thus conclude the Song.
" Holy and good art Thou, Lord God of Hoft,
" And all thy Works are wonderful and juft·
" Both Life and Death are in thy pow'rful Hand,
" Both Life and Death obey thy great Command

" By

" By thy great Pow'r the Heav'ns and Earth are aw'd;
" Then let the Heav'ns and Earth adore their GOD.
" Thou glorious Sun, that measur'st all our Days,
" Rising and setting, still advance his Praise:
" Thou Moon, and ye less glitt'ring Orbs, that dance
" Round this terrestrial Globe, his Praise advance.
" Ye seas, for ever waving to and fro,
' Praise, when ye ebb, and praise him when ye flow:
" Ye wand'ring Rivers, and each purling Stream,
" As ye pursue your Course, his Praise proclaim
" Ye Dews, and Mists, and humid Vapours, all,
' Praise, when ye rise; and praise him, when ye fall.
" But chiefly *Israel*, who dost daily view
" His pow'rful Works, his daily Praise renew "

GRATITUDE. A PASTORAL.

MENALCAS, COLIN.

MENALCAS.

FRiend COLIN! well o'ertook. I have of late
Observ'd thy chearful Mien, and airy Gait:
Say, what auspicious Change, since t'other Day,
When by thy lonely Cot I took my Way?
Sorrow and Sadness then o'erspread thy Brows,
And ev'ry Look did gloomy Cares disclose.
Now Joys diffusive in thy Aspect rise,
And Mirth and Gladness sparkle in thy Eyes.

E 2 COLIN.

COLIN.

Where haft thou liv'd, MENALCAS, not to know,
Whofe gen'rous Bounty has remov'd my Woe?
I thought, the gracious CAROLINA's Name,
Ere this, had fill'd the founding Trump of Fame.

MENALCAS.

That gracious Name, the World is bound to blefs,
All grateful Swains her gen'rous Deeds confefs.
But, COLIN, fay, has fhe remov'd thy Care?
I'm happy, when thy Happinefs I hear.

COLIN

O You, MENALCAS, know my abject Birth,
Born in a Cot, and bred to till the Earth
On rigid Worldlings always doom'd to wait,
Forc'd at their frugal Hands my bread to get ·
But when my Wants to CAROLINE were known,
She blefs'd me with a Pafture of my own.
This makes new Pleafures in my Bofom glow,
Thefe joyful Looks I to her Bounty owe.

MENALCAS

And may kind Heav'n reward that gracious Queen,
Who to thy Wants has fo propitious been!
Yet, tho' her Bounty has thy Wants fupply'd,
Let not her Bounty e'er exalt thy Pride,
But keep an humble Mind, a grateful Heart,
Her Favours far exceed thy own Defcit
Heav'n mov'd the Goodnefs of the Royal Dame;
And Heav'n and She thy Gratitude muft claim.

COLIN.

When me She first into her Favour took,
I cut this oaken Staff, ('tis now my Crook)
And grav'd her Royal Bounty in the Rind;
But grav'd it deeper in my grateful Mind:
The Letters in the Staff may wear away,
Those written in my Soul shall ne'er decay.

MENALCAS.

So may thy little Flock increase their Tale;
So may thy Field of Pasture never fail,
May Heav'n and She, in just Proportion, still
Or smile, or frown, as thou art good, or ill.

COLIN.

May hungry Foxes kill my tender Lambs,
May pois'nous Serpents suck their bleating Dams;
And may my Cows distended Udders fail,
Elude my Hopes, and never fill the Pail;
In short, (to make my Curse the more complete,
Tho 'tis the only Thing I dread and hate)
May Heav'n and heav'nly CAROLINE remove
Their Smiles, if COLIN e'er ungrateful prove.

MENALCAS.

Thy Thanks and Pray'rs her gen'rous Soul will please;
A Tribute justly due, and paid with Ease
Sometimes a Song, perhaps, she may require;
And thou to sing, but lately didst aspire,
When in an abject, low, laborious State,
Sunk deep in Cares, and press'd beneath their Weight:

E 3   Then

Then (fo, at leaft, 'tis faid among our Swains)
In Sonnets COLIN charm'd away his Pains
Much fooner now thou may'ft a Song rehearfe,.
Whene'er fhe condefcends to hear thy Verfe.

COLIN

O Friend! too well you know, my fimple Strains
Are far inferior to each rural Swain's.
Yet, fince Great CAROLINA thinks no Scorn,
To patronize a Shepherd meanly born,
Henceforth I'll ftrive to raife my Voice fublime,
And with her Royal Name adorn my Rhyme,
I'll on each verdant Mountain fing her Praife,
And vocal Groves fhall echo to my Lays,
To ev'ry Swain her Godlike Worth proclaim,
Nor ever drop the pleafing glorious Theme.

MENALCAS

Then, fince we're met, where friendly Branches
    fpread,
And trembling Leaves diffufe a cooling Shade;
Since, on the Sprays, the Thrufh and Finch rejoice,
Invoke thy Mufe, and tune thy rural Voice.

COLIN.

Another Day my rural Voice I'll raife,
Another Day the Mufe fhall tune her Lays:
But now, alas! fuch crowding Joys I find,
No Words can fpeak the Tranfports of my Mind.
Would PHOEBUS warm me with poetic Fire,
Or would the *Mantuan* Mufe my Tongue infpire;
As great ELIZA fhone in SPENCER's Line,
The Greater CAROLINA fhould in mine;
Then would I emulate the tuneful Throng,
And with her glorious Name immortalize my Song

On a GOOD CONSCIENCE.

THE folid Joys of human Kind
   Are thofe that flow from Peace of Mind;
For who the Sweets of Life can tafte,
With Vice, and tim'rous Guilt, oppreft?
'Tis Virtue foftens all our Toils,
   With Peace our Confcience crowns;
Gives Pleafure, when our Fortune fmiles,
   And Courage, when it frowns,
Calms ev'ry Trouble, makes the Soul ferene,
Smooths the contracted Brow, and chears the Heart
    within.

While guilty Minds, involv'd with Woe,
   Anticipate the future Blow,
Which is (to make Damnation more complete)
The leffer Hell, in Paffage to the great;
Bold and intrepid honeft Men appear;
For, as they know no Evil, none they fear
A glorious Shield of Virtue guards their Breaft;
Arm'd with themfelves, they always walk at Reft.

Thus, under burfting Clouds, and ftormy Skies,
   When Thunder roars, and Lightning flies.
   Th'Imperial Eagles boldly rove,
   Nor dread the fiery Bolt of JOVE;
While meaner Birds in fecret creep below;
And trembling fear, and often feel the Blow.

On RICHMOND PARK, *and* ROYAL GARDENS.

OF blifsful Groves I fing, and flow'ry Plains:
Ye Sylvan Nymphs, affift my rural Strains.
Shall *Windfor* Foreft gain a deathlefs Fame,
And grow immortal as the Poet's Name,
While not a Bard of all the tuneful Throng,
With thefe delightful Fields adorns his * Song?
Thy Gardens, *Richmond*, boaft an equal Theme,
And only afk an equal Mufe's Flame.
What tho' no Virgin Nymphs, of CYNTHIA's Train,
With Belt and Quiver grace the verdant Plain?
What tho' no fabled confecrated Floods
Flow o'er thy Fields, or murmur thro' thy Woods?
My Song thy real Beauties fhall purfue,
And paint the lovely Scenes, and paint 'em true;
A pleafing Tafk! Nor flight fhall be thy Praife,
It Royal CAROLINE accept thy Lays.

Delighted, often thro' the mazy Groves,
The Mufe, in penfive Contemplation, roves;
Or climbs the flow afcending † Hill, whofe Brow
Hangs o'er the filver Stream, which rolls below,
Where all around me fhining Profpects rife,
And various Scenes invite my gazing Eyes,
And, while I view one Object with Delight,
New pleafing Wonders charm the feafted Sight.
Now

---

* This was writ in the Year 1731, fince when, great Alterations and Improvements have been made in the Gardens, and feveral Poems publifh'd on the fame Subject.
† *Richmond* Hill.

Now this allures, now that attracts it most ;
And the first Beauty's in the second lost.

Thus, in a grateful Concert, may we hear
The Sounds at once surprize, and charm our Ear ;
The trembling Notes, in hasty Fugues, arise ,
And this advances, e'er the former flies ,
All seem to be confus'd yet all agree,
To perfect the melodious Harmony.

Beneath the Mount, with what majestic Pride
The Sire of Rivers rolls his silver Tide ,
Let Poets sing of *Hermus*' golden Shore.
His amber Foam, and Sands of shining Ore
Nor *Tagus* envy we, nor fruitful *Nile*,
Whose fatt'ning Floods enrich the thirsty Soil :
Happy BRITANNIA boasts as fair a Stream,
As great in Bounties, and as great in Fame ,
Since DENHAM's deathless Muse has sung his Tide,
And *India*'s Riches o'er his Surface glide.

Obsequious River, when my Eyes survey
Thy Waves, or East, or West, pursue their Way :
Now swiftly roll, to meet the briny Main ,
At stated Periods, now return again ;
How vain the Schemes of Infidels appear !
How Weak their Reas'nings, and the GOD how clear !
Say, Atheists, since you own, by Nature's Laws,
There's no Effect produc'd without a Cause ;
Why should the restless Stream run to and fro,
And, with alternate Motion, ebb and flow ;
Did not some Being, of superior Force,
Rule the wild Waves, and regulate their Course ?

Hence lofty *Windsor* to the Sight appears ,
And high in Air, her pompous Turrets rears :

Wide,

Wide, round her Domes, the spacious Forest shines
Tho' brighter much in POPE's harmonious Lines:
O! wou'd his tuneful Muse my Breast inspire,
With equal Warmth, with her sublimer Fire,
Then *Richmond* Hill renown'd in Verse shou'd grow,
And *Thames* re-echo to the Song below,
A second *Eden* in my Page shou'd shine,
And MILTON's *Paradise* submit to mine.

Oft, lost in Thought, forgetful of my Way,
I, o'er the Park, thro' Wilds of Beauty stray;
Where sportive Nature wantons at her Will,
And lavishes her Bloom, uncheck'd by Skill.
Old venerable Trees, majestic, rise,
Sublime in Air, and brave the vaulted Skies!
Which, free from cruel Steel, or Lab'rer's Hand,
In peaceful Age, and hoary Honour stand.
Here, when AURORA first begins to dawn,
The wakeful Larks spring mounting from the Lawn;
Pois'd by their Plumes, in lofty Flights they play,
With joyful Warblings, hail the approaching Day
But, when the Sun displays a purple Scene,
And drinks the pearly Dew, that deck'd the Green;
A thousand tuneful Birds in Concert meet.
A thousand tuneful Notes the Groves repeat;
And, when their Music ceases with the Day,
Sweet PHILOMELA chants her pensive Lay.

But, hark! I hear a louder Music found;
From Woods and Vales the various Notes rebound
'Tis *Albion*'s KING pursues the Royal Chace.
The nimble Stag skims o'er th'unbending Grass.
The Way which Fear directs, he trembling tries;
Nor knows, where Fear directs, or where he flies.
A Hundred diff'rent Sounds assail his Ears,
A Death, in ev'ry diff'rent Sound, he fears

And

And now he faintly moves a flower Pace,
And clofer now the Hounds purfue their Chace,
Till, in Defpair, back on his Foes he turns,
Makes feeble Efforts with his branchy Horns ;
Short is the Combat, foon he yields his Breath,
And gafping falls, and trembling pants, in Death.

Now to a fofter Theme defcends my Mufe,
Thro' artful Walks her pleafing Path purfues,
Where lofty Elms, and conic Lindens rife,
Or where th'extenfive Terras charms her Eyes,
Where Elegance and noble Grandeur meet,
As the Ideas of its Miftrefs, great,
Magnificently fair, majeftically fweet
See, on it's Margin, Fields of waving Corn,
Where bearded Crops, and Flow'rets this, adorn,
CERES and FLORA lovingly embrace,
And gay Varieties the Landfcape grace.

Hence lead me, Mufes, thro' yon arched Grove,
Adorn'd with Sand below, and Leaves above,
Or let me o'er the fpacious Oval trace,
Where verdant Carpets fpread the lovely Place,
Where Trees in regular Confufion ftand,
And fylvan Beauties rife on ev'ry Hand
Or bear me, Nymphs, to the fequefter'd Cell,
Where BOYLE and NEWTON, mighty Sages ! dwell ;
Whofe Fame fhall live, altho' the Grot decay,
Long as thofe facred Truths their Works difplay.

How fweetly pleafing is this cool Retreat,
When PHOEBUS blazes with meridian Heat !
In vain the fervid Beams around it play,
The rocky Roof repels the fcorching Ray,
Securely guarded with a fylvan Scene,
In Nature's Liv'ry dreft, for ever green.

To

To vifit *this*, the curious Stranger roves,
With grateful Travel thro' a Wild of Groves;
And, tho' directed, oft miftakes his Way,
Unknowing where the winding Mazes ftray;
Yet ftill his Feet the magic Paths purfue,
Charm'd, tho' bewilder'd, with the pleafing View,

    Not fo attractive lately fhone the Plain,
A gloomy Wafte, not worth the Mufe's Strain;
Where thorny Brakes the Traveller repell'd,
And Weeds and Thiftles overfpread the Field;
Till Royal GEORGE, and heav'nly CAROLINE,
Bid Nature in harmonious Luftre fhine;
The facred *Fiat* thro' the Chaos rung,
And Symmetry from wild Diforder fprung

    So, once, confus'd, the barb'rous Nations ftood,
Unpolifh'd were their Minds, their Manners rude;
Till *Rome* her conqu'ring Eagles wide difplay'd,
And bid the World reform——The World obey'd.

    How blefs'd the Man in thefe delightful Fields,
New Pleafures each indulgent Moment yie'ds
Let gayer Minds in Town purfue their Joys,
Exchanging Quietnefs for Crowds and Noife;
Confume the Night at Mafquerade or Play,
Or wafte, in bufy Idlenefs, the Day.
I envy not *Augufta*'s pompous Piles,
Since rural Solitude more pleafing fmiles.
O Solitude! the Sage's chief Delight!
What Numbers can thy lovely Charms recite!
Hail, peaceful Nymph! thou eldeft Thing on Earth
Nay, like Eternity thou hadft no Birth.
The Heav'ns alone can thy Commencement tell,
Ere MICHAEL fought, or peccant Angels fell;

Before

Before the Skies with radiant Light were clad,
In awful Gloom, and venerable Shade,
The FATHER thee his sole Companion made.
When to Creation first his Thoughts inclin'd,
And future Worlds were rising in his Mind,
He sat with thee, and plann'd the mighty Scheme:
With thee adjusted the stupendous Frame,
Contriv'd how Globes, self-balanc'd in the Air,
With restless Rounds shou'd rule the circling Year,
How Orbs o'er Orbs in mystic Dance should roll,
What Laws support, and regulate the Whole.
Nor art thou yet impair'd, celestial Dame,
Thy Charms are still attractive, still the same;
With thee the Mind, abstracted from the Crew,
May study Nature, and her Ends pursue,
With thee I hear the feather'd Warblers sing,
With thee survey the Beauties of the *Spring*,
When Blossoms, Leaves, and Fruits the Branches yield,
And *Eden*'s Glory crowns the happy Field.

Here first the Muse (auspicious was the Place!
Rejoic'd to see her Royal Guardian's Face
How mil'd, yet how majestic, was her Look!
How sweetly condescending all she spoke!
On ev'ry pleasing Accent Wisdom hung,
And Truth and Virtue dwelt upon her Tongue.
O! were I equal to the glorious Theme,
Then should my Lays immortalize her Fame;
Or paint Great GEORGE in peaceful Laurels dreft,
With *Albion*'s Safety lab'ring in his Breast;
Who (while contending Nations round him jar,
And Subjects Wealth supports their Monarch's War)
Guards happy *Britain*, with his floating Tow'rs,
From purple Slaughter, and invading Pow'rs;
No plund'ring Armies rob our fruitful Plain,
But, bless'd with Peace and Plenty, smiles the Swain.

Not

Not fo he fmiles upon the foreign Shores;
But ftarving walks thro' Nature's lavifh Stores;
Poor Peafants with their rigid Burdens groan,
And till the Glebe for Harvefts not their own.
What, tho' their more propitious PHOEBUS fhines
With warmer Rays, and chears the curling Vines?
What, tho' rich Olives grace the fertile Soil,
And the hot Climate teems with fatt'ning Oil?
The hungry farmer views his Crops in vain,
In vain the Vineyard tempts the thirfty Swain,
While their ftern Tyrant's arbitrary Pow'r
Rifles the Plains, and ravages their Store.
Thy Sons, BRITANNIA, from fuch Evils free,
Enjoy the Sweets of Peace and Liberty;
A gracious Sov'reign fmiles upon the Throne,
And Heav'n confirms the happy Realm his own.

AVARO and AMANDA.

A POEM, in FOUR CANTOS,

Taken from the Spectator, VOL I. NUMB. XI.

CANTO I.

WHAT Ills from Want of Educations flow,
From Avarice what cruel Scenes of Woe,
I mean to fing; except the tuneful Maid
Neglect my Numbers, and refufe her Aid.

Say,

Say, Goddess, first, what made the Youth explore
A foreign Clime, and quit his native Shore ?
Say too, how on the barb'rous Isle he came,
What mov'd the Kindness of the *Negro* Dame ?
What cou'd provoke a faithless Youth to sell
A Friend, whose only Crime was loving well ?

Now had AVARO twenty *Winters* pass'd,
His blooming Features ev'ry Beauty grac'd ;
In silver Rings, his loosely flowing Hair
Hung o'er his Shoulders with a comely Air ;
Robust his Limbs, and daring was his Soul,
And Vigour crown'd the well proportion'd Whole :
His graceful Charms the Ladies oft survey'd,
And oft their Eyes an am'rous Signal made ;
But never could the tender Passion move,
The stubborn Youth was still averse to Love ;
Yet, tho' his Breast was Proof to CUPID's Dart,
A more ignoble God enslav'd his Heart.

No Mysteries of Faith disturb'd his Head ;
For Mysteries of Faith he seldom read ;
That moral Law, which Nature had imprest,
He blotted from the Volume of his Breast ,
Yet in his Mind his Father's Precepts bears,
Who often rung this Lesson in his Ears .
Wou'd you, my Son, to Happiness aspire,
Know, *Gold,* alone can Happiness acquire ,
He that has *Gold,* is pow'rful as a King,
Has Valour, Virtue, Wisdom, ev'ry Thing !
This to obtain, your utmost Skill bestow,
And if you gain it, be not careful how .
If in the Court, or Camp, you take Delight,
Then dare to flatter *there,* or *here* to fight
Or, shou'd the Merchant's Life your Fancy please,
Be bold, and bravely venture on the Seas ,

" Many

" Many by Merchandize have gain'd Renown,
" And made the *Indies* Wealth become their own '
The Youth imbib'd the Precepts of his Tongue,
Neg'ecting ev'ry Law of Right and Wrong,
Taught by his Sire to court deftructive Gain,
He burns to try his Fortune on the Main.

    While other Youths, by Wit or Pleafure fway'd
Frequent the Play, the Ball or Mafquerade;
AVARO, ftudious, in his Chamber ftays,
Careless of Balls, of Mafquerades, and Plays,
There adds, fubftracts, and, with unweary'd Pain,
Learns all the Rules of Int'reft, Lofs, and Gain.

    Next, from an old Aftronomer, he tries
To learn the Planets Journey thro' the Skies ;
With *him*, at Night, when Heav'n ferene appears,
He points the Quadrant at the fhining Spheres ;
The HYADES, and frozen Pole furveys,
Which guide the Sailor o'er the diftant Seas ;
Then Maps and Models of our Globe prepares,
And carefully infpects both Hemifpheres ;
From Eaft to Weft he views the fpacious Round,
Pleas'd with the Modern World COLUMBUS found
In Hope elate, the Youth impatient ftands,
And feems to grafp both *Indies* in his Hands.
This fees the Sire, and haftily provides
A Veffel, Proof againft the Winds and Tides.
The Youth embarks, the foft propitious Gales
Arife, and foon expand the fwelling Sails,
The Ship glides fwiftly o'er the liquid Plain,
And NEPTUNE fmiles, and courts him on the Main.

    But fee, how Mortals are the Sport of Fate !
How oft unhappy, ftriving to be great !
Ere CYNTHIA twice her monthly Race had run,
An Omen of the fatal Storm begun.

                         The

The murm'ring Wind arises by Degrees,
And rocks the Ship, and sweeps the curling Seas;
Now louder, with impetuous Force it roars,
And shoves the swelling Surges to the Shores;
Till rapid Rain, and Flakes of bick'ring Flame,
With dreadful Thunder vex th'etherial Frame.
Struck with Surprize, the tim'rous Merchant stands,
Nor knows what he forbids, or what commands:
Nor safely back, nor can he forwards go;
But trembling waits, and fears the fatal Blow.

Long Time the Sailors work against the Wind,
With fruitless Toil, to gain the Port assign'd;
Till Courage, Hope, and all Provisions fail'd,
And fear, Despair, and Want their Souls assail'd.
Forc'd by the Storm into a winding Bay,
Their joyful Eyes an *Indian* Isle survey;
When straight they quit their Ship, and gain the Shore,
And for Recruits the savage Land explore.

Adjoining to the dreary Beach, there stood
Wild Shrubs and Trees, that form'd a gloomy Wood;
Where, close obscur'd, the crafty Natives lay,
And watch'd the wand'ring Crew remote from Sea:
Then forth they rush, and strait their Bows prepare,
Too late the Sailors see th'approaching War:
In vain the Brave engage, or Tim'rous fly,
The Tim'rous and the Brave, promiscuous die;
The barb'rous Fields are stain'd with purple Gore,
And dreadful Groanings echo to the Shore.
Our youthful Merchant 'scapes, and flies alone,
His Fear impels, and Safety prompts him on,
Thro' dusky Woods he takes his trembling Flight.
The dusky Woods conceal him from their Sight,
Till in the devious Wilds, remote from Foes,
Then, on the Ground, he weeping vents his Woes;

Oft

Oft curs'd his haplefs Fate, and often thought
On what the hoary Star-monger had taught,
How, at our Birth, as diff'ient Planets rule,
They form a Wit, or conftitute a Fool;
How, in the Maze of Life, we act, as they
Attract, retard, or force us in the Way.
And, as he thefe uncertain Cenfures made,
Againft the Stars he, thus exclaiming, faid·

The Planets fure fome noxious Pow'r difplay,
And rule my Life with arbitrary Sway,
Elfe I had ne'er forfook my native Home,
Nor in this baleful Defert met my Doom——
And yet, when I reflect, I cannot fee,
How Globes infenfible fhould influence me!
I chufe my Actions, when the Choice is made,
I nor invoke, nor yet confult their Aid.
When Mortals act according to their Will,
Can Heav'n be call'd the Author of their Ill?
Too late I find, the Stars are not in Fault,
But 'tis that golden Wifh my Sire has taught
Enticing *Gold*, that damn'd deceiving Guide,
Induc'd me firft to ftem the foaming Tide,
Fallacious *Charm*, that led me from Repofe,
Now leaves me in a Labyrinth of Woes.

So, when compacted Vapours, in the Night,
Skim o'er the Fields, with a delufive Light,
The injudicious Traveller furveys
Th'alluring *Scene*, and courts the glift'ring Blaze;
Till, tempted o'er a Rock's impending Biow,
He falls to fome tremendous Gulph below.

Thus the unhappy Youth laments his Fate,
Confcious of all the Ills that round him wait,

Till

Till setting PHOEBUS leaves the blushing Sky,
And glimm'ring Stars a feeble Light supply·
The Shades of Night increase his anxious Care,
And add a greater Horror to Despair.

CANTO II.

ALL Night in Tears the pensive Merchant lay,
  And often wish'd, and fear'd the coming Day ;
Till, on the Hills, the rising Sun display'd
His golden Beams, and chas'd away the Shade :
Harmonious Birds salute his chearful Rays,
And hail the rosy Morn with joyful Lays,
While, stretch'd upon the Ground, AVARO moans,
Answ'ring their tuneful Songs with piercing Groans.

  Not distant far from where the Youth was laid,
A purling Stream, in pleasing Murmurs, play'd.
And, by the Margin of the crystal Flood,
Two Rows of Trees in beauteous Order stood ;
Whose Branches form'd a pendant Arch above,
Diffusing gloomy Verdure o'er the Grove.
An *Indian* Princess hither daily came,
Pleas'd with the grateful Shade, and cooling Stream :
She now was walking to her lov'd Retreat,
And heard the mourning Youth lament his Fate
Fix'd in Amaze a-while she list'ning stood,
Then swift approach'd him, rushing thro' the Wood.
Th'affrighted Merchant rose with gazing Eyes,
And tim'rous Looks, that testify'd Surprize.

Back-

Backward he ftarts ; the Dame, with equal Fears,
Recedes as faft, and wonders what appears ;
Yet, bolder grown, fhe foon advanc'd again,
Smit with the Beauty of the Godlike Man .
His Drefs, and fair Complexion, charm'd her Sight;
Each glowing Feature gave her new Delight ,
While Love and Pity both arofe within,
And kindled in her Soul a Flame unfeen.
With equal Joy AVARO now furvey'd
The native Graces of the *Negro* Maid ·
He view'd her Arms, with various Ribbands bound;
Her downy Head, with painted Feathers crown'd ,
With Beades, and lucid Shells, in Circles ftrung,
Which fhone refulgent, as they round her hung.

As when, in fplendid Robes, a courtly Maid
Begins the Dance at Ball or Mafquerade,
The Pearls and Di'monds fhine with mingled Light,
And glitt'ring Pendants blaze againft the Sight.

So fhone the beauteous Shells around her Waift,
And fparkling Gems, that deck'd her jetty Breaft ,
All which AVARO's gazing Eyes purfue,
Charm'd with her lovely Shape, difclos'd to View :
Each Limb appears in juft Proportion made,
With Elegance thro' ev'ry Part difplay'd ·
And now his Cares diffolve, new Paffions move ;
And Nature intimates, the Change is LOVE.

Not far remote, a cooling Grot was made,
In which the Virgin often fought a Shade
Thick Shrubs, and fruitful Vines around it grew ,
And none, except herfelf, the Manfion knew.
To this obfcure *Recefs* the Royal Dame,
Rejoicing, with her lovely Captive came ·
Then, from the Branches, with officious Hafte,
She plucks the Fruits, which yield à fweet Repaft ·

That

That done, she, with her Bow, explores the Wood ;
Pierc'd with her Shaft, the Fowl refigns his Blood.
Then back she haftens to her cool Retreat,
And for AVARO drefs'd the grateful Meat ·
To flake his Thirft, she next directs his Way,
Where cryftal Streams in wild Meanders ftray,
Nor lets him there, expos'd to Foes, remain,
But to the Cave conducts him fafe again.

So doats AMANDA on the Merchant, while
She fcorns the *Lovers* of her native *Ifle*
For all the Heroes of her Country ftrove,
With Emulation, to attract her Love,
And, when they could the painted Fowls infnare,
Or pierce the favage Beaft in fylvan War,
The Skins and Feathers, Trophies of their Fame,
They gave for Prefents to the Royal Dame ;
All which she to her lov'd AVARO brought,
And with them gayly deck'd his shining Grot :
The fpotted Panther here she hung, and there,
With Paws extended, frown'd the shaggy Bear ;
Here gaudy Plumes appear, in Luftre bright,
There Shells and Pearls diffufe a fparkling Light.

As when, to grace fome Royal Prince's Hall,
The skilful Painter animates the Wall,
Here warlike Heroes frown in martial Arms,
There a foft Nymph difplays her blufhing Charms ;
A pleafing Landfcape next invites our Eye,
And the Room glows with fweet Variety.

Yet, ftill to give her Lover more Delight,
(Left what he daily faw, should pall the Sight)
When SOL with Purple cloath'd the Weftern Sky,
And Shades extended shew'd the Ev'ning nigh,
She to fome verdant Grove the Youth convey'd,
Where Nightingales harmonious Mufic made

Soft

Soft Flow'rets were their Couch; and, all around,
Diffusive Sweets perfum'd the fragrant Ground.
There oft she would his snowy Bosom bare,
Oft round her Fingers wind his silver Hair,
Charm'd with the Contrast, which their Colours made,
More pleasing than the Tulip's Light and Shade.
Nor was the Youth insensible, but soon
Repaid her Love by shewing of his own
Oft would his Bosom heave with speaking Sighs,
Oft would he gaze, and languish with his Eyes;
Now on her panting Breast his Head repose,
To meet his Head her panting Breast arose;
While in her Soul ecstatic Raptures glow'd,
And her fond Arms believ'd they clasp'd a God.

So liv'd the happy Pair, observ'd by none,
Till both had learn'd a Language of their own,
In which the Youth, one Ev'ning in the Shade,
Beguiles the harmless unsuspicious made,
Leans on her Breast, and, with a Kiss, betrays;
Then vents his specious Fraud in Words like these:

Witness, ye Gods, and all ye bless'd above,
(For ye can witness best, how well I love)
If e'er among our blooming Nymphs, I knew
Such Pleasures, as my Soul receives from you?
O dear AMANDA! could I but, with thee,
Once more my happy native Country see,
You should not there in lonely Caves retreat,
Nor trace the burning Sands with naked Feet;
Your Limbs, which now the Sun and Wind invade,
Should neatly be in softest Silks array'd,
In gilded Coaches gayly should you ride,
By Horses drawn, which prancing Side by Side,
Neigh, foam, and champ the Bit with graceful Pride,
Our Time, in Pomp and Peace, should slide away,
And blooming Pleasures crown the smiling Day,

And when the setting Sun forsook the Skies,
Approaching Night should but increase our Joys :
We would not on the chilling Ground embrace,
Nor Foes, as now, should interrupt our Peace ;
But both reposing on some easy Bed,
Soft, as the fleecy Down, that decks thy Head,
The sportive God of Love should round us Play,
While we, in Raptures, pass'd the Night away.
Then let us carefully, my dear, explore
The Haven, where I first approach'd the Shore.
Perhaps we shall some floating Ship survey,
Safe to conduct us o'er the watry Way :
Nor let the foaming Waves your Steps retard ;
I'll guard you o'er, and be a faithful Guard.

How oft, alass ! is Innocence betray'd,
When Love invites, and Flatterers persuade ?
How could the Dame, a Stranger to Deceit,
Imagine such a heavenly Form a Cheat ?
She paus'd, she sigh'd, then, with a pensive Look,
Half loth, and half consenting, thus she spoke :

Once has AVARO 'scap'd the raging Main :
Why would you tempt the fickle Seas again ?
To seek new Dangers, when in Safety here,
Would but provoke the Deities you fear ———
Sometimes, I own, we've been surpriz'd by Foes,
Whose nightly Walks have wak'd you from Repose.
Yet still I guard your sacred Life secure,
And always will———What can AMANDA more ?

Thus said, she clasp'd him in her loving Arms,
Embrac'd his Neck, and doated on his Charms :
And now both shew their Passions in their Look,
And now Connubial HYMEN both invoke ;

In

In fportive Joys they clos'd the genial Day,
While PHILOMELA fung the Nuptial Lay;
Till foon the Youth reclin'd upon her Breaft,
And golden Slumbers feal'd their Eyes to Reft.

C A N T O III.

SOON as the Sun began to gild the Day,
And on the Hills emit a trembling Ray,
AMANDA, from her flow'ry Bed awoke,
Sad was her Heart, and difcompos'd her Look;
The briny Torrent flows adown her Cheeks,
While thus fhe to her dear AVARO fpeaks.

O Thou, on whom my Life and Love depend,
If e'er AMANDA claim'd the Name of Friend,
If e'er I gave thy troubled Mind Repofe,
Or hid thee, when purfu'd with furious Foes;
Explain this *Dream*, that terrifies my Breaft;
The ftrangeft, Fear, or Fancy e'er impreft!

Methought a God defcended from the Skies;
Celeftial Beauty fparkled in his Eyes;
Like Rays of PHOEBUS fhone his radiant Hair,
His Shape like thine, like thine his graceful Air;
A Robe was neatly girt about his Waift,
Fine as my lov'd AVARO's filken Veft,
His fhining Lips upon my Breaft he laid,
And foftly prefs'd my Hand, and fmiling faid:

" An"

" Arife, my Dear, my lov'd AMANDA rife;
" An eafier Lodging waits thee in the Skies.
" I am defcended from the bleft Abodes,
" To bear thee hence to Heav'n among the Gods;
" No Enemies fhall there difturb thy Reft;
" There, with thy *Lover*, live for ever bleft."

Thus faid, he rais'd me from the dewy Plain,
And bore, or feem'd to bear me, o'er the Main:
But foon he led me to a diftant Ifle,
Where Horrors reign, and Comforts never fmile:
Thick Brakes and Brambles choak'd the dreary Coaft,
The only Product, which the Land could boaft;
Till a dejected, fervile Race arofe,
With gloomy Sadnefs brooding on their Brows:
This Crowd, promifcuous, with inceffant Toil,
Or rooted up the Wood, or plow'd the Soil:
How each perform'd his Tafk, a Tyrant view'd;
And fternly fhook his Whip, and menac'd as he ftood.
Sometimes to fhun the direful Lafh, they fled,
Th'infulting Lord purfu'd with greater Speed:
Sure not fo fearful fly the trembling Bears,
To fhun our Hunters Darts, and miffive Spears;
Sure not fo fwift our Hunters e'er purfu'd
The trembling Bears, when flying thro' the Wood;
As from the Tyrant's Wrath they fwiftly run,
Or, as the Tyrant, fwifter urg'd them on.
Each to his wonted Tafk he drove again,
And made *me* mix among the fervile Train;
Doom'd with the reft to groan beneath the Yoke,
Alike I felt the dire correcting Stroke.
But, O! what added moft to my Defpair,
My Godlike Guide was falfe, and left me there——

As thus fhe fpake, confus'd her Looks appear'd;
For ftill her Soul the dreadful Vifion fear'd.

Deciding

Deciding Reafon from her Seat withdrew,
And Fancy painted all the Scene anew.
The Youth to chear the drooping Dame eſſay'd,
When ſtrait a Boar came ruſhing thro' the Shade ;
The craſhing Woods proclaim'd his rapid Force,
While two fleet Youths purſu'd the ſylvan Courſe.
The Lovers ſtarted from their flow'ry Seats,
Surpriz'd , and each a diff 'rent Way retreats.

As when ſome Muſquet's Thunder has expell'd
Two loving Turtles from the verdant Field ,
Both, diverſe, thro' the wide ethereal Plain
Fly ſwift ; and flying, fear their Mate is ſlain.

So parting, devious fled th'affrighted Pair ;
Such was AVARO's, ſuch AMANDA's Fear.
The foaming Boar between 'em ſwiftly paſt,
The nimble Courſers urge the Chace as faſt ,
Till ſoon they pierce him with a mortal Wound ;
He falls, and purple Gore diſtains the Ground :
Then, from the ſavage War, they take their Way,
And to the Cave, triumphant, bear the Prey.

Soon as the ſportive Hunters left the Wood,
The loving Pair conceal'd no longer ſtood ,
But trembling both forſook the duſky Shade,
Both trembling met upon the op'ning Glade ·
Mute with Surprize a-while they ſtood ; the Man
Broke Silence firſt, and thus his Tale began

O dear AMANDA ! ſoon we have ſurvey'd
This myſtic Viſion of the Night diſplay'd .
Theſe are the frowning Tyrants in thy Dream,
That chas'd the Slaves, and we their flying Game.

Some

Some Part, said she, resembled this, I own;
And some remains a Riddle yet unknown:
What meant that God, which still, methinks, I view?
That radiant Deity! so much like You!
And what the Fields above, which he propos'd?
Say, if the Mystery can be disclos'd?

To whom the Youth· Our active Fancy seems
For ever roving, roving most in Dreams.
For then the Soul, disburden'd of her Load,
Soars high, and grows prophetic, like a God;
Minds Things when past, as present to our View
And, by Allusion, knows the future too.
Thus, when to Sleep your musing Head reclind,
She kept our Ev'ning Converse in her Mind,
Reflected on the Joys my Country yields,
Joys, sweet as those in yonder azure Fields;
Till soaring higher, striving to discern
Her hidden Fate, and future Fortune learn,
Heav'n shew'd her something like this Morning Chace,
By trembling Slaves, who fled their Tyrant's Face,
Perhaps to warn us timely from our Bed,
For, O my dear AMANDA! had we staid,
I had not liv'd to tell this mystic Tale,
Nor you, to hear the Secrets I reveal——
But let us to my happy Country steer,
Nor longer wait impending Ruin here.

So spake the Youth, and, with a gracious Look,
He seem'd to sanctify the Words he spoke

Go, she reply'd, go where you are inclin'd,
Your faithful Lover will not stay behind.
If o'er the Seas you shall attempt your Way,
The Seas shall not compel me here to stay,
Nor will I fear the Surges of the Deep,
(For Surges oft, you say, assail the Ship)

G 2   Calm

Calm and compos'd, intrepid, will I ſtand,
Till you conduct me to your native Land.
Or, if you wou'd ſome other Clime purſue,
Then ſhall ſome other Climate pleaſe me too.
And when the happy deſtin'd Land we meet,
Where Providence ſhall fix our wand'ring Feet,
With joyful Servitude, I'll ſtill attend
On you, my nuptial Lord, and deareſt Friend.
Soon as AURORA ſpreads her purple Ray,
When you awake to chace the nimble Prey,
I'll alſo riſe, and, with an equal Art,
Diſplay the Net, or ſpeed the pointed Dart;
Or ſearch the Plains, and taſteful Herbs provide;
Or ſtrip the Vines, and preſs their juicy Pride.
Each Ev'ning will I fondly deck your Bed
With ſweeteſt Flow'rets gather'd from the Mead,
And when, diſſolv'd in downy Sleep, you lie,
I'll wake and watch if Foes approach too nigh
To guard your Life, all Hazards will I run,
And, for your Safety, ſacrifice my own.

    To whom the Youth   No Hazards ſhall you run;
Nor, for my Safety, ſacrifice your own;
Nor yet at Ev'ning fondly deck my Bed
With ſweeteſt Flow'rets, gather'd from the Mead;
Nor ſhall AMANDA taſteful Herbs explore,
Nor ſhall AVARO chaſe a ſavage Boar
A ſofter Bed, than Flowers, ſhall give you Reſt;
A choicer Meat, than Fruits, indulge your Taſte,
Ten Thouſand Things my grateful Soul ſhall find?
To charm your Fancy, and delight your Mind;
I'll vary Love a hundred different Ways,
And inſtitute new Arts to make it pleaſe:
So ſhall our future Race of Children ſee
A conſtant Proverb made of you and me·
When *Britiſh* Youths ſhall court the doubting Dame,
And want Expreſſions equal to their Flame,

Then,

Ther, ftrongly to atteft it, fhall be faid,
" *True as* AVARO *to the* Indian *Maid.*"

To whom AMANDA, (paufing at the *Name*)
What meant AVARO by the *doubting Dame* ?
Has any of your *Britifh* Damfels made
A *Doubt* of what fuch godlike Being faid ?
Or is it cuftomary to your Clime ?
Has ever Youth committed fuch a *Crime,*
As *bafe Ingratitude* ? Has any there
Deluded firft, and then forfook the Fair ?
I cannot think, your Love will e'er decline,
Nor can my radiant Angel queftion mine.
By yon bright Beams, which paint the rifing Day;
By thy bright Charms, as beautiful as they;
By all our pleafing Hours of Love, I vow
To fhare your Fate thro' ev'ry Scene of Woe;
Content, with you, to yield my vital Breath;
For Life, without you, would but lengthen Death:

With fuch fweet Talk their Moments they beguile;
Both feem impatient for the deftin'd Ifle:
He daily vows, and daily is believ'd;
She daily hears, and daily is deceiv'd.

CANTO IV.

FArewel, bright Goddefs of th'*Idalian* Grove;
Farewel, ye fportive Deities of LOVE !
No longer I your pleafing Joys rehearfe,
A rougher Theme demands my penfive Verfe;

A

A Scene of Woes remains to be difplay'd,
Indulgent Love with Slavery repaid .
Ingratitude, and broken Vows, and Lies,
The mighty Ills that fpring from Avarice,
Provoke my Lays   Your Aid, ye Mufes, bring ;
Affift my Tragic Numbers, while I fing.
Say, what enfu'd, when, on the briny Deep,
The watchful Dame beheld a floating Ship ?
She call'd, and beckon'd to it from the Shore ,
Then to the Youth the grateful Tidings bore ;
And faid, I fomething fee like winged Trees,
(Strange to behold !) fly fwiftly o'er the Seas ,
Their bulky Roots upon the Billows float
Say, is not this the Ship, you long have fought ?
Or I miftake, or, by the Gods Command,
This comes to bear us to your native Land :
Then haften, fee the Partner of your Heart,
With You, her Guide, is ready to depart ,
My Father, Mother, Friends, I bid Adieu,
Friends, Father, Mother, not fo dear as *You*.

To whom the Youth, with fmiling, Brow, reply'd:
O thou true Pattern of a faithful Bride !
Who dar'ft thy Father, Mother, Friends refign ;
And rifque thy own dear Life, to refcue mine ! ——
If I forget the Debt I owe to *Thee*,
May all the Gods forget their Care of *Me*.
In more wild Deferts let me rove again ,
Nor find a Friend, like *Thee*, to eafe my Pain !
There let the Vultures, Wolves, and Tigers tear
This Body, *Thou* haft kindly nourifh'd here !

So faying, to the Beach he ftraight defcends :
And, by the Flag difcerns the Crew his Friends .
And now his Heart exults within his Breaft ,
His loving Mate an equal Joy confeft ;

She,

She, with him, gladly ventures on the Main,
Unthinking of her future Toil and Pain.

So, to the Plough, the Heifer, yet unbroke,
Walks chearful on, nor dreads th'impending Yoke;
Till, in the Fields, urg'd with the piercing Goad,
She groans, and writhes, reluctant with her Load.

The *British* Bark was to *Barbadoes* bound.
Th'expected Shore the Sailors quickly found;
Where, safe from Danger, now the perjur'd Youth,
False to his former Vows of sacred Truth,
Reflecting, counts the Int'rest he had lost,
While Fate detain'd him on the *Indian* Coast:
The frugal Thoughts suppress his am'rous Flame,
And prompt him to betray the the faithful Dame.
Yet scarce he can the cursed Fact pursue,
But hesitates at what he fain wou'd do:
For, tho' his Av'rice moves him to the Ill,
His Gratitude within him struggles still;
And 'twixt two Passions, neither guides his Will.

As when two Scales, with equal Loads suspend,
Sway to and fro; alternate both descend,
Till, undecling, each aloft abides;
Nor this, nor that, the doubtful Weight decides.

So stood the doubtful Youth a-while, nor wou'd
Forsake the Evil, nor pursue the Good;
Till, as the Sailors in the Haven stay,
To purchase Slaves, the Planters croud the Key:
One asks, for what the *Negro* may be sold;
Then bids a Price, and shews the tempting Gold:
Which when AVARO views with greedy Eyes.
He soon resolves to gain th'alluring Prize.
Nor Oaths, nor Gratitude, can longer bind;
Her Fate he thus determines in his Mind:

" Suppose

" Suppofe I fhould conduct this *Indian* o'er ;
" And thus, inftead of Gold, import a *Moor* ———
" Would not my Sire, with ftern contracted Brows
" Condemn my Choice, and curfe my nuptial Vows?
" Was it for this I learn'd the Merchant's Art?
" Only to gain a doating *Negroe*'s Heart!
" Was it for this the raging Seas I croft?
" No, Gold induc'd me to the *Indian* Coaft,
" And Gold is offer'd for this fimple Dame,
" Shall I refufe it, or renounce my Flame? ———
" Let am'rous Fools their tirefome Joys renew,
" And doat on *Love*, while *Int'reft* I purfue."
He added not; for now, intent on Gold,
And dead to all Remorfe, the *Dame* he fold.

AMANDA ftood confounded with Surprize,
And filently reproach'd him with her Eyes.
She often try'd to fpeak, but when fhe try'd,
Her Heart fwell'd full, her Voice its Aid deny'd;
And, when fhe made her fault'ring Tongue obey,
Thefe Words, commix'd with Sighs, found out their
        Way.

" Who can the myftic Ways of Fate explain?
" Am I awake, or do I dream again;
" Is *this* the fad Reward of all my Care?
" Was it for this I cheer'd thee in Defpair?
" The Gods above, (if any Gods there be)
" Witnefs what I have done to fuccour thee!
" Yet, if my *Kindnefs* can't thy Pity move,
" Pity the *Fruits* of our unhappy *Love*.
" Oh! let the Infant in my pregnant Womb,
" Excite thee to revoke my threaten'd Doom!
" Think how the future Slave, in Climes remote,
" Shall curfe the treach'rous Sire, that him begot."

So spake the mourning Dame, but spake in vain;
Th'obdurate Youth insults her with Disdain;
Not all her Kindness could his Pity move,
Nor yet the *Fruits* of their unhappy *Love.*
But, as the Flames, which soften Wax, display
The same warm Force to harden sordid Clay,
That Motive which would melt another Heart,
More harden'd his, and made him act a double Vil-
    lain's Part.
He, for the Child, demands a larger Sum;
And sells it, while an Embryo in the Womb.

And now he sternly takes her by the Hand,
Then drags her on, reluctant to the Land,
While, as she walks her dismal Fate she moans,
The Rocks around her echo to her Groans
' O base, ungrateful Youth! she loudly cries;
' O base, ungrateful Youth! the Shore replies:
' And can'st thou, cruel, perjur'd Villain! leave
' Thy tender Infant too, an abject Slave,
' To toil, and groan, and bleed beneath the *Rod?*
' Fool, that I was, to think thou wert a God!
' Sure from some savage Tiger art thou sprung——
' No! Tigers feed, and fawn upon their Young.
' But thou despisest all paternal Cares,
' The Fate of Infants, and their Mothers Pray'rs.''

In vain she does her wretched State deplore;
Pleas'd with the Gold, he gladly quits the Shore;
The ruffling Winds dilate the Sails, the Ship
Divides the Waves, and skims along the Deep.
Three Days the bellying Canvas gently swells,
Clear shines the Sun, and friendly blow the Gales;
Then frowning Clouds invest the vaulted Sky,
And hollow Winds proclaim a Tempest nigh:
Fierce BOREAS loudly o'er the Ocean roars,
Smoke the white Waves, and sound the adverse Shores;
                  While,

While, to increafe the Horrors of the Main,
Defcends a Deluge of impetuous Rain.
The giddy Ship on circling Eddies rides,
Tofs'd, and re-tofs'd, the Sport of Winds and Tides.
Redoubled Peals of roaring Thunder roll
And Flames, conflicting, flafh from Pole to Pole,
While guilty Thoughts diftract AVARO's Soul.
Of Life defpairing, tho' afraid to die,
One fatal Effort yet he means to try ·
While all the bufy Crew, with panting Breath,
Were lab'ring to repel the liquid Death,
AVARO from the Stern the Boat divides,
And yields up to the Fury of the Tides
Tofs'd on the boift'rous Wave, the Veffel flies,
Now finking low, now mounting to the Skies,
Till foon the Storm decreas'd, and, by Degrees,
Hufh'd were the Winds, and calm the ruffled Seas,
The Sailors fafely fteer their Courfe again,
And leave AVARO floating on the Main,
Who landed quickly on a lonely Ifle,
Where human Feet ne'er print the baleful Soil,
A dreary Wildernefs was all appear'd,
And howling Wolves the only Sound he heard;
A thoufand Deaths he views before his Eyes,
A thoufand Guilt-created Fiends arife,
A *confcious-Hell* within his Bofom burns,
And racks his tortur'd Soul while thus he mourns

    " Curs'd be the Precepts of my felfifh Sire,
" Who bad me after fatal Gold afpire !
" Curs'd be myfelf, and doubly curs'd, who fold
" A faithful Friend, to gain that fatal Gold !——
" O ! could thefe gloomy Woods my Sin conceal,
" Or in my Bofom quench this fiery *Hell*,
" Here would I pine my wretched Life away,
" Or to the hungry Savage fall a Prey.——

               " But

" But can the gloomy Woods conceal my Sin,
" Or cooling Shadows quench the *Hell* within?
" No; like some Spirit banish'd Heav'n, I find
" Terrors in ev'ry Place, to rack my Mind,
" Tormenting conscious Plagues increase my Care,
" And guilty Thoughts indulge my just Despair——
" O! where shall I that piercing Eye evade,
" That scans the Depths of Hell's tremendous Shade!"

So Saying, straight he gave a hideous Glare,
With rolling Eyes, that witness'd strong Despair:
Then drew his pointed Weapon from the Sheath,
Confus'dly wild, and all his Thoughts on Death,
To pierce his trembling Heart he thrice essay'd,
And thrice his coward Arm deny'd its Aid
Mean while a howling Wolf, with Hunger prest,
Leap'd on the Wretch, and seiz'd him by the Breast;
Tore out his Heart, and lick'd the purple Flood,
For Earth refus'd to drink the *Villain's* Blood.

On the Hon. Mrs. HORNER's *Travelling*
for the Recovery of her Health.

CLARISSA long has sought, in vain,
Physicians Aid, to ease her Pain;
But now their Aid she seeks no more,
Nor longer will their Drugs endure:
Spite of their Art, her Spirits fail,
Her Cheeks are turn'd a languid Pale;

Yet,

Yet, tho' her mortal Part's decay'd,
Her nobler *Virtue* does not fade;
Her Soul inflexible to Ill,
In Piety advances still
So Metals lie in chymic Fires;
And, while the grosser Part expires,
The Flames refine the golden Ore,
And make it brighter than before.

She now a warmer Clime explores,
To prove the Air of foreign Shores.
O! may the temp'rate Breezes bring
Salubrious Med'cines on their Wing ·
Thou, PHOEBUS, too, propitious shine;
And, (since the Power of Physic's thine)
Send blooming Health on ev'ry Beam,
Dispel her Pains, and chear the Dame:
Else must my melancholy Strain,
In mournful Elegies, complain.
Ev'n now, too well, these Numbers show,
My drooping Fancy's damp'd with Woe.
Yet, tho' my Verse deserves no Praise,
Let no four Critic damn my Lays;
Since OVID's self but faintly fung,
When only Grief inspir'd his Tongue.

The ABSENT LOVER.

ALEXIS, walking in the Park,
Met CHLOE, just before 'twas dark:
He ask'd a Kiss, nor she deny'd,
I don't know what they did beside:

But,

But, as a Child, in Thought, chews o'er
The Sweatmeats which he eat before,
So in his Mind ALEXIS keeps
The dear Impreſſion of her Lips:
He felt it all the following Day,
At Night indulg'd it at the Play;
One ling'ring Act he muſing ſtay'd,
But knew not what the Actors ſaid;
He thought the Park in *Drury-Lane,*
Believ'd the Nymph appear'd again,
He ſeems to view her ſnowy Neck,
Her ruby Lip, and roſy Cheek,
Her graceful Smiles, and ſparkling Eyes,
Her panting Boſom fall and riſe·
And now he claſp'd her in his Arms,
(Twas all imaginary Charms)
When, riſing to the Height of Bliſs,
His Lips eſſay'd to take a Kiſs,
An Orange wench trod on his Foot;
And ſcreaming, "*Will you have ſome Fruit?*"
Surpriz'd, he dropt the pleaſing Theme,
And found his Joys a waking Dream,
He ſwore, and wept, and kick'd the Wench,
Forgot his Hat, and left the Bench.

On a Screen, *work'd in Flowers by* Her Royal
Highnefs *ANNE, Princefs of* ORANGE.

ILLUSTRIOUS Nymph! whofe Art could raife,
    This fkilful Monument of Praife,
Forgive the Bard, who ftrikes the Lyre;
Accept the Verfe, your Toils infpire:
For, when your Labours ftrike my Eyes,
The voluntary Numbers rife.
Who can be filent, when they view
This fair Creation wrought by *You?*
Each Flow'r does with fuch Luftre fhine,
Such Beauties crown the gay Defign,
That Nature fix'd in wonder ftands,
To fee fhe's rival'd by your Hands;
And, jealous of your Art, difplays
A Blufh, when fhe the Work furveys.
Yet this accomplifh'd Piece, we find,
Shews a faint Image of your *Mind,*
The lovely Charms, and Graces *here,*
But copy thofe that centre *there.*

To D E A T H.

An I R R E G U L A R O D E.

HAIL, formidable KING!
    My Mufe thy dreadful Fame fhall fing.
Why fhould old HOMER's pompous Lays
Immortalize ACHILLES' Praife!

Or why should ADDISON's harmonious Verse
  Our MARLBRO's nober Deeds rehearse?
  Alas! no more these *Heroes* shine,
  Their Pow'r is all subdu'd by *Thine*.
  Where are these mighty *Leaders* now,
Great POMPEY, CÆSAR, and Young AMMON too,
  Who thought he drew immortal Breath
  These bold ambitious Sons of MARS,
  Who dy'd the Globe with bloody Wars,
Are vanquish'd all by thee, victorious DEATH!

II.

Ev'n while they liv'd, their Martial Hate
  But firmer fix'd thy Throne;
Nor, tho' it hasten'd others Fate,
  Could it delay their own.
Nor didst thou want *their Rage* to kill;
Thy own can execute thy Will:
Whene'er thou dost exert thy Pow'r,
A Thousand morbid Troops thy Call obey;
  Sometimes thy wasting Plagues devour,
  And sweep whole Realms away.
Now with contagious Biles the City mourns,
  And now the scorching Fever burns,
  Or trembling Quartan chills,
Of Heat and Cold the dire Extremes
Now freeze, now fire the Blood with Flames,
  Till various Torment kills.

III.

Consumptions, and Rheumatic Pain;
And Apoplectic Fits, that rack the Brain;
Soul panting Asthmas, Dropsy, and Catarrh,
Gout, Palsy, Lunacy, and black Despair,

Pangs,

Pangs, that neglected Lovers feel ;
Corroding Jealoufy, their earthly Hell,
 Which makes the injur'd Woman Wild ;
And pow'rful Spleen that gets the *Man* with Child;
Phyficians, Surgeons, Bawds, and Whores, and Wine,
Are all obfequious Minifters of *Thine* ,
 Nay, and RELIGION too,
When Hypocrites their Intereft purfue,
 Or frantic Zeal infpires,
 It calls for Racks, and Wheels, and Fires :
Then all our myftic Articles of Faith,
Inftead of faving Life, become the Caufe of DEATH.

III.

Great MONARCH ! how fecure muft be thy Crown,
When all thefe Things confpire to prop thy Throne?
 Yet, in thy univerfal Reign,
 Thou doft not ufe tyrannic Sway.
 Whate'er the Weak and Tim'ious fay,
  Who tremble at thy Frown;
 Thou art propitious to our Pain,
And break'ft the groaning Pris'ner's Chain,
  Which Tyranny put on.
 In *Thee* the Lover quits his Care,
 Nor longer couits the cruel *Fair,*
  Her Coldnefs mourns no more ·
In *Thee* Ambition ends its Race,
And finds at length the deftin d Place,
 It ne'er could find before :
 The Meichant too, who plows the Main,
  In greedy Queft of Gain,
 By Thee to happier Climes is brought,
Than thofe his wild, infatiate Av'rice fought.

V.

V.

Propitious Succourer of the Distrest,
Who often, by the Dead, dost make the Living blest!
How could profusive *Heirs* attend
   Their Mistress, Bottle, Ball, and Play,
If timely *Thou* wert not their Friend.
   To snatch the scraping Sire away?
How would dull Poets weary Time
   With their insipid Rhyme,
And teaze and tue the the Reader's Ears
   With Party Feuds and Paper Wars,
If *Thou*, great Critic! didst not use
Thy Pow'r, to point a Period for their Muse?
   The Bard, at thy decisive Will,
   Discards his *mercenary Quill*,
   Then all his mighty Volumes lie
Hid in the peaceful *Tomb* of vast Obscurity.

VI.

I, like the rest, advance my Lays;
With uncouth Numbers, rumble forth a Song,
   Sedately dull, to celebrate thy Praise;
And lash, and spur the heavy lab'ring Muse along:
   But soon the fatal Time must come,
   (Ordain'd by Heav'n's unerring Doom)
   When Thou shalt cut the vital Thread,
And shove the verbal Embryos from my Head.
   Then, since I'm sure to meet my Fate,
   How vain would *Hope* appear?
   Since *Fear* cannot protract the Date,
   How foolish 'twere to *fear?*
   I'll strive, at least, to stand prepar'd,
   Thy Summons to obey;
   Nor would I think thy Sentence hard,
   Nor wish, nor fear the *Day*;
But live in conscious Peace, and die without Dismay.

VII.

VII.

Fallacious Reas'ners wrong *Thee*, when
  They call thy Laws fevere.
Severe to whom ? *To wicked Men*.
  Then let the Wicked fear.
  Thou judgeft all with equal Laws,
  No venal Witnefs backs thy Caufe,
    No Bribes to *Thee* are known ,
  If thy impartial Hand but ftrike,
  The Prince and Peafant fall alike,
    The Courtier and the Clown.
  What tho' a while the Beggar groans,
  While Kings enjoy their guded Thrones ?
What are Diftinctions, Pomp, and Regal Train, ⎫
And *Honours*, got with Care, and kept with Pain ?⎬
One friendly Stroke of *Thine* fets level all again. ⎭
  All earthly Grandeur muft decline ,
Nay, ev'n Great GEORGE's Pow'r fubmit to *Thine*.
  But *thy Dominion* fhall endure,
  Till PHOEBUS meafures Time no more :
Then all fhall be in dark Oblivion caft,
And ev'ry mortal Kingdom fall , but thine fhall fall
    the laft.

T R U T H

TRUTH and *FALSHOOD.*

A FABLE.

SOON as the Iron Age on Earth began,
And Vice found easy Entrance into Man;
Forth from her Cave infernal *Falshood* came;
Falshood, the Hate of Gods, of Men the Shame:
A silken Robe she wore, of various Hue,
Its Colour changing with each diff'rent View.
Studious to cheat, and eager to beguile,
She mimick'd *Truth*, and ap'd her heav'nly Smile;
But mimick'd *Truth* in vain; the varying Vest,
To ev'ry searching Eye, the Fiend confest.

At length she saw celestial *Truth* appear.
Serene her Brow, and chearful was her Air;
Her silver Locks with shining Fillets bound,
With Laurel Wreaths her peaceful Temples crown'd:
A Lilly Robe was girded round her Waist
And, o'er her Arms, a radiant Mantle cast:
With decent Negligence, it hung behind,
And loosely flowing, wanton'd in the Wind.
Thus *Truth* advanc'd, unknowing of Deceit;
And *Falshood*, bowing low, began the Cheat:

Hail, charming Maid, bright as the Morning Star,
Daughter of JOVE, and Heav'n's peculiar Care!
Tis thine to weigh the World in equal Scales,
And chide the conscious Soul, when Vice prevails,
Dispensing Justice with impartial Hand,
The mightiest Pow'rs submit to thy Command:
Ev'n God's themselves, tho' in their Actions free,
Consult, resolve, and act, as you decree:

Great

Great Sov'reign Jove, the firſt Ethereal Name,
Advis'd with thee to form the heav'nly Frame:
As *Truth* approv'd, he bad the Fabric riſe,
And ſpread the Azure Mantle of the Skies,
Plac'd ev'ry Planet in its proper Sphere,
Nor rolls *this* Orb too wide, nor *that* too near——
But why thus walk we, mindleſs of our Eaſe,
Expos'd beneath the Sun's meridian Blaze?
Better retire, and ſhun the ſcorching Ray,
Till fanning *Zephyrs* cool our Ev'ning Way.
Hear how yon limpid Streams run murm'ring by,
And tuneful Birds their ſylvan Notes apply,
See fragrant Shrubs along the Borders grow,
And waving Shades beneath the Poplar Bough;
All theſe invite us to the River's Side,
To bath our Limbs, and ſport within the Tide:
So cool the Stream, the flow'ry Bank ſo ſweet,
Diana's Self might covet the Retreat.
Nor can a ſhort Diverſion check your Haſte;
Freſh Strength will ſoon ſucceed ſuch welcome Reſt,
As rapid Currents, held a-while at Bay,
With ſwifter Force purſue their liquid Way.

So ſpake the Phantom; and, with friendly Look
Supporting what ſhe ſaid, approach'd the Brook.
Truth follow'd, artleſs, unſuſpicious Maid!
And, in an evil Hour, the Voice obey'd.
Both, at the cryſtal Stream arriv'd, unbound
Their diff'rent Robes, both caſt them to the Ground
The Fiend, upon the Margin, ling'ring ſtood,
The naked Goddeſs leapt into the Flood:
Sporting, ſhe ſwims the liquid Surface o'er,
Unmindful of the matchleſs Robe ſhe wore.
Not *Falſhood* ſo — She haſty ſeiz'd the Veſt,
And with the beauteous Spoils herſelf ſhe dreſt:
Then, wing'd with Joy, outflew the ſwifteſt Wind,
Her own infernal Robe far left behind.

Straight

Straight she aspires above her former State,
And gains Admittance to the Rich and Great:
Nay, such her daring Pride, that some report,
When thus equipp'd, she boldly went to *Court*:
There spake and look'd with such a graceful Air,
Mistaken *Fame* pronounc'd her wise and fair.
She fill'd the Wanton's Tongue with specious Names,
To deal in *Wounds*, and *Deaths*, in *Darts*, and *Flames*;
He prefac'd all his leud Attempts with Love,
And *Fraud* prevail'd, where *Reason* could not move.
At length she mingled with the learned Throng,
And turn'd the Muses mercenary Song.
In all the Labyrinths of Logic skill'd,
She taught the subtle Reas'ner *not* to yield;
Instructed how to puzzle each Dispute,
And boldly *baffle* Men, tho' not *confute*.
Now, at the Bar, she play'd the Lawyer's Part;
And shap'd out *Right* and *Wrong* by Rules of Art;
Now, in the Senate, rais'd her pompous Tone,
Talk'd much of *Public Good*, but meant *her own*.
Oft to th'*Olympian* Field she turn'd her Eyes,
And taught the Racers how to gain the Prize.
In Schools and Temples too she claim'd a Share,
While *Falshood*'s Self admir'd her Influence there.

Deluded *Truth* observ'd the Fraud too late,
Nor knew she to repair a Loss so great.
In vain her heav'nly Robes, she, sighing, seeks;
In vain the humid Pearls bedew her Cheeks,
In vain she tears the Laurel from her Hair,
While Nature seems to sympathize her Care:
The glowing Flow'rs, that crown th'enamel'd Meads,
Weep fragrant Dews, and hang their drooping Heads,
The sylvan Choirs, as conscious of her Pains,
Deplore her Loss in melancholy Strains.
Thus, pensive and uncloath'd, upon the Shore
She stands, and sees the Robe, which *Falshood* wore:

Detested

Detefted Sight ! nor longer now fhe mourns,
But, Grief to Rage transform'd, with Anger burns·
Into the Stream, the hellifh Robe fhe toft,
And fcorn'd a Habit, fo unlike the loft.

Hence *Truth* now naked roves, as in Difgrace,
None, but the Wife and Virtuous, fee her Face
From Cities far fhe modeftly retreats,
From bufy Scenes of Life, to peaceful Seats;
Is chiefly found in lonely Fields and Cells,
Where Silence reigns, and Contemplation dwells.
Hence *Falfhood* cheats us in the fair Difguife,
And feems *Truth*'s Self to all unwary Eyes;
'Triumphs and thrives, in Pow'r, and Wealth, and Fame,
And builds her Glory on her Rival's Name;
With Safety dares to flatter, fawn, and footh;
For who knows *Falfhood*, when array'd like *Truth* ?

On *Two young Ladies leaving the Country.*

SAY, lovely Nymphs ! who fly from rural Sweets,
To noify Crouds, thick Air, and fmoky Streets,
Do Balls, or Plays, your graceful Steps invite ?
Can Balls, or Plays, like *Richmond* Groves, delight ?
No tuneful PHILOMEL, in Town, complains,
To charm your lift'ning Ear with vary'd Strains,
No fragrant Gales refrefh the fick'ning Fields,
No chearful flow'ry Scenes the City yields.
But Mifts, and lambent Fogs, where-e'er you pafs,
Shall cloud the Graces that adorn your Face,

While

While those bright Eyes, like sully'd Gems, appear,
Or Stars, just glimm'ring thro the dusky Air.

Nor will you only Change of Beauty find;
Illusive Scenes will mock your pensive Mind.
In cloudless Mornings, when you've drank your Tea,
And read a Page in Sherlock, or in —— GAY ;
Perhaps your Thoughts, transported, here may rove,
And, to your Mind, present the blissful Grove.
You'll think to walk by silver *Thames*'s Shore ;
Or trace the verdant Mead, as heretofore,
When at the Door, the rural Vision flies,
Smoak, Coaches, Fops, and Carmen meet your Eyes :
Straight back you'll turn, vex'd with the fruitless Search ,
Bid * ROBERT call a Chair, and go to *Church.*

On MITES. *To a* LADY.

'Tis but by Way of Simile.　　　PRIOR.

DEAR Madam, did you never gaze,
Thro' Optic-glass, on rotten *Cheese* ?
There, Madam, did you ne'er perceive
A Crowd of dwarfish Creatures live ?
The little Things, elate with Pride,
Shut to and fro, from Side to Side ·
In tiny Pomp, and pertly vain,
Lords of their pleasing Orb, they reign ;

And

* The Footman.

And, fill'd with harden'd Curds and Cream,
Think the whole Dairy made for *them*.

So Men, conceited Lords of all,
Walk proudly o'er this pendent Ball,
Fond of their little Spot below,
Nor greater Beings care to know ;
But think, thofe *Worlds*, which deck the Skies,
Were only form'd to pleafe their Eyes.

CLOE's CONQUEST.

'TWAS by a purling Stream, beneath a Shade
Young CLOE, CUPID, and ALEXIS play'd
LOVE's Goddefs, with her Doves, fat looking on;
And, fmiling, nodded to her wanton Son :
Her wanton Son his keeneft Arrow drew :
Swift, to the Swain, the pointed Weapon flew :
Inflexible to *Love*, the Shepherd ftood,
Repell'd the Shaft, and mock'd the baffled God;
Till CLOE rais'd her Eyes with killing Art,
And fhot him with a more pernicious Dart :
Your's is the Victory, ALEXIS cries ;
Not CUPID's Shaft has kill'd, but CLOE's Eyes.

On C E L I A's Picture, *drawn by Sir*
Godfrey Kneller.

WITH such a sapient Eye, and heav'nly Mind,
  MINERVA taught her Arts to hum'n Kind;
With such attractive Charms, and graceful Air,
VENUS was judg'd the *Queen* of all the *Fair*
Such Sense and Beauty to the *Painter* shone,
He drew *Two* Goddesses to finish *One.*

On Delia *singing, and playing on Music.*

I.

WHEN DELIA tunes her vocal Song,
  And strikes the trembling Strings ;
The list'ning Audience round her throng,
  Admiring, while she sings.

II.

But, when we view the skilful *Fair,*
  We're struck with more Surprize ;
Before, she only pleas'd our Ear,
  But now, inchants our Eyes.

III.

Beauty and Harmony combin'd,
  Like secret Charms betray ;
Like Ghosts in magic Rings confin'd,
  We cannot stir away.

I   IV.

IV.

So Birds, imprudent fall to Ground,
  When pleasing Notes they hear,
Charm'd with the Piper's artful Sound,
  Till taken in his Snare.

A Description of a JOURNEY

To Marlborough, Bath, Portsmouth, &c.

To the Right Honourable the Lord Viscount

PALMERSTON.

WHILE some, my Lord, the *Roman* Coast
      explore,
Survey the Fanes, and trace their Beauties o'er.
Studious of Arts, by which ingenious BOYLE,
Now draws the Plan, or now erects the Pile;
More bounded in my Fancy, and my Purse,
I, o'er domestic Plains, pursue my Course;
And ev'ry pleasing Object in the Way,
The Muse shall sing, if you accept her Lay.

When

When CANCER fiercely glow'd with PHOEBUS'
    Heat,
And Clouds of Dust flew ev'n in *Brentford-Street*;
O'er *Hounslow-Heath* my early Course I steer,
For Robbers fam'd; but I no Robbers fear.
Let Gold, like Guilt, increase the *Miser's* Grief;
A *Poet's* Purse, like *Virtue*, dares a Thief.
Colebrook I quickly pass, and soon my Eyes
Survey the Royal Tow'rs of *Windsor* rise:
Charm'd with the Theme of POPE's harmonious Song,
I check my Steed, and slowly move along;
As ling'ring Mariners contract their Sails,
To feast on Odours of *Arabian* Gales.
But left, my Lord, your Patience should accuse
The dull Narration of a tedious Muse,
I will not sing each Trifle that occur'd,
How much I eat, and drank, and whip'd and spurr'd:
How oft my Palfry stumbled in the Way,
Till * *Hatford* ends the Travel of the Day;
Where kind † MENALCAS, Partner of my Soul,
Revives me with his friendly, flowing Bowl;
Yet forces no intemp'rate Bumpers round,
Except when DELIA's Health the Glasses crown'd.
A thousand Labours past, we now run o'er,
What Scenes we acted, and what Toils we bore:
No Party Feuds, nor Politics we name;
The Joys of Friendship mostly were our Theme.
Warn'd by the Clock, we' now retire to Rest,
Till rising PHOEBUS streak'd the purple East.
Breakfast soon o'er, we trace the verdant Field,
Where sharpen'd Scythes the lab'ring Mowers weild:
Straight Emulation glows in ev'ry Vein;
I long to try the curvous Blade again.

I 2   As

---

* A little Village, near *Farringdon* in *Berks*.
† A Farmer, once the Author's Master, and still his Friend.

As when, at *Hockley-hole*, old Gamesters view
Young Combatants their Martial Sports renew,
A youthful Vigour fires their antient Soul,
Nor former Wounds their Courage can controul; ,
Again they mount the Stage, again they play,
Again they bear the noble Prize away.
So with Ambition burns my daring Breast,
I snatch the Scythe, and with the Swains contest;
Behind 'em close, I rush the sweeping Steel,
The vanquish'd Mowers soon confess my Skill.

  Not long at this laborious Sport I stay;
But, with my Friend, to * *Charlton* take my Way.
'Tis there, my Lord, induc'd by potent Ale,
Swains leave their Ploughs, and Threshers quit their
          Flail:
Your † Bounty soon provokes the Bells to ring,
Clowns dance, Boys, hollow, and hoarse Coblers sing.
Not greater was the Joy in antient *Greece*,
When Æson's Son produc'd the *Golden Fleece*,
Than now appears in ev'ry *Thresher's* Breast,
Soon as your *Gold* sings Prologue to the Feast.

  Why should the Muse recite our Bill of Fare,
And with a long Description tire your Ear?
None can your gen'rous Treat with Want reproach;
All eat enough, and many drank too much.
Full twenty *Threshers* quaff around the Board;
All name their Toast, and ev'ry one, *my Lord*.
No Cares, no Toils, no Troubles now appear;
For Troubles, Toils, and Cares are drown'd in *Beer*;
Till soon the chol'ric Fumes of Liquor rise,
Flush in their Face, and sparkle in their Eyes:
They now the rustic Feats of Manhood boast,
Who best could reap, or mow, or thresh the most
                                      Con

* Where the Author liv'd a *Thresher*.
† Money which his Lordship sent to treat the *Threshers*.

Contention doubtful ! All with Anger burn,
While each appears a Hero in his Turn .
Hard Words fucceed , fo far can *Beer* prevail,
That Blows are menac'd e'en without a Flail ;
Till thus our Landlord, rifing from his Chair,
Like prudent NESTOR, ftops impending War:

" What Madnefs, Friends, what Madnefs can
　" engage
' Your Minds to burn with this unfeemly Rage ?
' For fhame, ftain not with Blood our grateful Chear ;
' Defift from *Blood* —— or elfe defift from *Beer.*
" Are thefe the only Thanks you give my Lord ?
' And is it thus his Favours you reward ?
' If no refpect you pay this chearful Feaft,
" Yet pay the nobler Founder fome, at leaft ——

He faid　Abafh'd the confcious Heroes ftood,
Shook Hands, and thirfted more for *Beer* —— than *Blood :*
Another Glafs to TEMPLE's Health they pour ,
And praife their Liquor much, his Bounty more.

Oft as this * *Day* returns, fhall *Threfhers* claim
Some Hours of Reft, facred to TEMPLE's Name ;
Oft as this *Day* returns, fhall TEMPLE chear
The *Threfhers* Hearts with Mutton, Beef, and Beer :
Hence, when their Childrens Children fhall admire
This Holiday, and, whence deriv'd, enquire ,
Some grateful Father, partial to my Fame,
Shall thus defcribe from whence, and how it came.

" Here, Child, a *Threfher* liv'd in antient Days ;
" Quaint Songs he fung, and pleafing Roundelays ;

I 3　　　　　　　　　　　　　　A

* 30th of *June,* on which his Lordfhip treats the *Threfhers* every
Year,

" A gracious QUEEN his Sonnets did commend;
" And some great Lord, one TEMPLE, was his *Friend*:
" That *Lord* was plea 'd this Holiday to make,
" And feast *the Threshers, for that Thresher's* Sake."

Thus shall Tradition keep my Fame alive,
The *Bard* may die, the *Thresher* still survive

Next, over *Pewsey's* fertile Fields I haste,
Fields with the bearded Crops of CERES grac'd !
While pleasing Hopes my grateful Bosom cheat,
But soon they vanish'd — * S I A N L E Y was not here.

From hence the Muse to silver *Kennet* flies,
On whose green Margin *Hertford's* Turrets rise.
Here often round the verdant Plain I stray,
Where † THOMPSON sung his bold unfetter'd Lay;
Or climb the winding, mazy ‡ Mountains Brow.
And tho' I swiftly walk, ascend but slow.
The spiral Paths in gradual Circles lead,
Increase my Journey, and elude my Speed:
Yet, when at length I reach the lofty Height,
Towns, Vallies, Rivers, Meadows meet my Sight ;
A thousand grateful Objects round me smile,
Whose various Beauties over-pay my Toil.

So may you often see the studious Youth
Begin the long, laborious Search for TRUTH ;
How slow his Progress, but how great his Pain !
How many mazy Problems vex his Brain.
Before he o'er the Hills of *Science* rise,
Where, far from vulgar Sight the Goddess lies !

Yet,

---

* Rev. Mr. *Stanley*, Rector of *Pewsey*, who first encouraged the
Author
  † Mr *Thomson* compos'd one of his *Seasons* here.
  ‡ *Marlborough* Mount.

Yet, there arriv'd, he ends the happy Chace;
Reflects, with Pleasure, on his glorious Race,
Sees the bright Nymph so many Charms display,
As crown the Labours of the lengthen'd Way.

Within the Basis of the verdant Hill,
A beauteous Grot confesses HERTFORD's Skill;
Who, with her lovely Nymphs, adorns the Place;
Gives ev'ry polish'd Stone its proper Grace;
Now varies rustic Moss about the Cell;
Now fits the shining Pearl, or purple Shell:
CALYPSO thus, attended with her Train,
With rural Palaces adorns the Plain;
Nor with more Elegance her Grots appear,
Nor with more Beauty shines th'*Immortal Fair.*

The Muse her Journey, next, to *Bath* pursues;
Bath, fix'd by Nature to delight the Muse!
Where flow'ry Shrubs, and curling Vines unite;
Hills, Vales, and waving Woods attract the Sight;
A vary'd Scene! For Nature here displays
A thousand lovely Charms, a thousand Ways·
ALLEN attends, to dress her beauteous Face,
With Handmaid Art improving ev'ry Grace;
Now forms the verdant Walk, or sunny Glade,
Or pours the Waters o'er the steep Cascade;
Or now contracts 'em with judicious Skill,
And leads 'em, gently murm'ring, down the Hill.

A Son of ÆSCULAPIUS here I meet,
Polite his Manners, and his Temper sweet:
His sage Discourse, with soft, persuasive Art,
Charm'd the pleas'd Ear, till it improv'd the Heart:
Bright *Truth*, and *Virtue*, were his lovely Theme,
Which seem'd more lovely, when describ'd by *him*.

Various

Various Diverfions here employ the *Fair*;
To Dancing fome, and fome to Play repair:
Not * MUSIDORA fo confumes her Days,
The Dame who bad me fing JEHOVAH's Praife:
Uncharm'd with all the flutt'ring Pomp of Pride,
Heav'n, and domeftic Care her Time divide:
In her own Breaft fhe feeks a calm Repofe,
And fhuns the crouded Rooms of *Belles* and *Beaux*,
Where COQUETILLA oft her Eyes has roll'd,
Oft won a worthlefs Heart, and loft her Gold.

From *Bath*, I travel thro' the fultry Vale,
Till *Sal'sb'ry* Plains afford a cooling Gale
Arcadian Plains where PAN delights to dwell,
In verdant Beauties cannot thefe excel.
Thefe two, like them, might gain immortal Fame,
Refound with CORYDON and THYRSIS' Flame,
If, to his Mouth, the Shepherd would apply
His mellow Pipe, or vocal Mufic try:
But, to his Mouth, the Shepherd ne'er applies
His mellow Pipe, nor vocal Mufic tries
Propt on his Staff, he indolently ftands,
His Hands fupport his Head, his Staff his Hands;
Or, idly bafking in the funny Ray,
Supinely lazy, loiters Life away.
Here, as I pafs'd the Plains, (a lovely Scene,
Array'd in Nature's Liv'ry, gaily green!)
On ev'ry Side the wanton Lambkins play'd,
Whofe artlefs Bleatings rural Mufic made;
Too harfh, perhaps, to pleafe politer Ears,
Yet much the fweeteft Tune the Farmer hears.

Soon as the Plains are ravifh'd from my Sight,
New diff'rent Profpects equally delight;

Where

* Mrs. STRNLEY, who defired the Author to write the *Su-nammite*.

Where * PEMBROKE's Turrets charm my gazing
  Eyes,
And awful Statues solemnly surprize ·
Bards, Sages, Heroes, Patriots, Princes stand,
A mixt, majestic, venerable Band !
Here mighty HOMER, PHOEBUS' eldest Son,
Or sings, or seems to sing, in breathing Stone.
See Martial PHOCION silently persuade,
And smooth tongu'd CICERO, in *Marble*, plead :
Here shines great POMPEY, greater JULIUS there,
With daring BRUTUS, honestly severe
Friendship, and *Freedom* in his Soul contend ;
Forgive him CÆSAR, if he wrong'd his Friend !
Tho' BRUTUS' Dagger pierc'd thy Bosom thro',
'Twas *Liberty*, not *Malice*, struck the Blow.
Unhappy BRUTUS, destin'd to withstand
Thy Friend's Ambition with a fatal Hand !
Unhappy CÆSAR, whose Ambition mov'd
That fatal Hand to murder whom it lov'd !
Had'st thou, like *Britain*'s Monarch, strove to save
Expiring Nations, not the World enslave,
Thy Laurels then had still unblasted stood,
Nor BRUTUS e'er been stain'd with CÆSAR's Blood.

Not far from hence, old *Sarum*'s Ruins stand,
High on a bleak and barren Tract of Land,
A Mount, which once sustain'd a City's Weight,
And lofty Tow'rs adorn'd its awful Height,
Till want of Water forc'd the thirsty Croud
To seek the Vale, where crystal Rivers flow'd.
There † POORE the first auspicious Work began ;
First, for a Temple drew the glorious Plan,
Then quickly makes the sacred Columns rise,
And bids the lofty Spire invade the Skies.
         The

* Earl of PEMBROKE's Seat at *Wilton.*
† Bishop POORE, who built the Cathedral.

The prudent People too, with equal Hafte,
New Dwellings built, which far their old furpaft.
Cautious of Thirft, they make the docile Tide,
In winding Currents, thro' the City glide.
In ev'ry Street the wanton NAIADS play,
To ev'ry Door their liquid Urns convey,
In which the lately thirfty Peafant fpies
At once the cooling Draught, and fcaly Fries;
Scenes, which, before, the lofty Mount deny'd!
Hence let Ambition learn to check its Pride
High Stations often bring a Weight of Cares,
True Happinefs is found in humble Spheres.
This ufeful Truth let _Sarum's_ Glory fhow,
Which faded when on high, but flourifhes below.

　　I next to BATHURST's * rural Seat afcend,
BATHURST, my infant Mufe's gen'rous Friend!
And, as around his fpacious Park I ftray'd,
Charm'd with the Profpect, which the Fields difplay'd
Mufing on Verfe, the willing Numbers came,
My Song began, and CLARENDON my Theme.
What fweeter Subject could I wifh to chufe?
What Scenes more lovely can delight a Mufe?
See, FLORA paints the Ground with vary'd Dyes,
And fragrant Shrubs with Odours fill the Skies!
Here curling Vines their lufcious Sweets difclofe,
There fair POMONA loads the blufhing Boughs.
See, fruitful CERES crowns the Vales with Corn,
And fleecy Flocks the verdant Hills adorn!
Here waving Trees project a cooling Shade,
Where BATHURST oft converfes with the _Dead_;
Reads over what the antient Sages wrote,
Nor only reads, but acts as Sages taught,
Improves the prefent Hour that Fortune gives;
Nor trufts To-morrow, but To day he lives.

As

* CLARENDON Park.

As thus my carelefs Lay, unlabour'd flows,
Before my Eyes a * Pile of Ruins rofe ;
Whofe rugged Walls, like native Rock-work fhone ;
For Time had turn'd the Cement into Stone.
Our Second HENRY here, if Fame be true,
Meafur'd the Prince's Right and People's Due :
Made Laws to bound the Priefts and Barons Claim—
Nor ev'n thofe Laws did haughty BECKET blame,
BECKET ! true Tyrant of the *Roman* State,
Curs'd with Religion juft enough to hate ;
Whofe ftern, ambitious Zeal his King defy'd,
And damn'd all thofe, who dar'd oppofe his Pride.

O Thou Supreme ! whofe Mercy ever fhone
The beft, the brighteft Jewel in thy Crown !
Never let me fuch cruel Faith approve,
Which bids me hate, when Heav'n commands to love;
Let Chriftian Charity incline my Mind
To wifh the Happinefs of all Mankind !
In focial Friendfhip always let me live,
Slow to be angry, eafy to forgive !

PAULTONS affords me next a kind Retreat,
Where crouding Joys my grateful Heart dilate;
To fee the Friend, who firft my Lays approv'd,
Who loves the Mufe, and by her is belov'd ;
Who taught her tender Pinions how to fly,
Told when fhe crept too low, or foar'd too high.
O STANLEY ! if, forgetful of thy Love,
I e'er to Gratitude rebellious prove ,
Still may I want a Friend, but never find :
May FORTUNE, PHOEBUS, STANLEY, prove unkind.

Here often thro' the gloomy Woods I rove,
Pleas'd with the filent Horror of the Grove.

And

* *King-Manor,* where the Conftitutions of CLARENDON were
made, See CAMDEN of *Wiltfhire.*

And now the Lawn, and winding Walks delight;
And now the *Memphian* Turret charms my Sight.
Here conic Firs in graceful Order stand;
'Tall Cedars there, the Growth of *Syrian* Land.
Lead me, ye sacred DRYADS! lead me thro'
Your sylvan Scenes, where future Navies grow;
Where lofty Oaks their branching Arms extend,
And tow'ring Pines to kifs the Clouds ascend;
Where op'ning Glades admit the sunny Ray,
Or venerable Groves exclude the Day.
There let me Knaves, and Fools, and Fops despise,
And think of Actions worthy of the Wife.

My Friend and me, *Southampton* next receives;
Southampton, wash'd with THETIS' silver Waves.
Upon whose sandy Margin * *Bevis* rears
His Head, on which a stately Dome appears;
Where *British* SCIPIO, crown'd with Martial Bays,
In Solitude enjoys his antient Days.
Yet, still inclin'd to conquer, wages here,
With stubborn Woods and Wilds, innoxious War,
Subdues the native Rudenefs of the Soil,
And makes the barren Sand with Verdure smile;
Bends the young Plant obedient to his Will,
Or thro' the Valley leads the cryftal Rill,
Sublimes the Mount, or bids the Mole subside,
To stretch the Profpect o'er the lucid Tide.
The Foils of Art illuftrate his Design;
And make the *Di'mond* NATURE brighter shine.

Charm'd with the Beauties of the silver Sea,
We board a Ship, and skim the watry Way
Blown with propitious Gales, we quickly view
BRITANNIA'S Strength, her Guard, and Glory too,
Where

* Mount *Bevis*, Seat of the Right Honourable the Earl of *Peterborough*, who was then living.

Where * GEORGE's dreadful Eagles waiting stood,
To bear his fatal Thunder o'er the Flood.
The wond'rous Scene delights my gazing Eyes,
At once imparting Pleasure and Surprize.
Intrepid Sailors, swarming in the Sky,
Intent on Business, diff 'rent Labours try:
Some stride the Yard, or tow'ring Masts ascend;
Some on the Ropes, in airy Crouds, depend,
Thick as the Insects, round the Poplar, play,
When Phoebus gilds 'em with a Western Ray.

But unexpected Dangers oft deceive
The daring Man, who tempts the foamy Wave:
While on the Fleet we all delighted gaze,
The sudden Winds arise, and sweep the Seas ;
With rapid Force they fly, and from the Ship,
Disjoin the Boat, and drive it o'er the Deep.
Our cautious Pilate quickly shifts the Sails,
Reverts his Course against the furious Gales.
O Chloe ! then what ruthless Pains distrest,
Thy dizzy Head, and rack'd thy tender Breast !
How often did the Bard thy Fate bemoan !
How often did he wish thy Pains his own !
How did the Tritons, mov'd with Pity, gaze
On thy fair Face, distorted twenty Ways !
Yet, tho' distorted, still thy Features show
Bright in Distress, and innocent in Woe.
So Venus oft her silver Light displays,
Thro' Ev'ning Mists, that rise to cloud her Rays.

But Neptune now, who pity'd Chloe's Pain,
Returns the Boat , we steer our Course again,
At Six, we safely land at *Portsmouth* Key,
And soon forget the Dangers of the Sea.
Straight to some hospitable Inn we haste,
Revive our Spirits with a sweet Repast:

K   The

* Spithead.

The fmiling Glafs, with rofy Liquor crown'd,
Sacred to friendly Healths, goes chearful round ;
While Time, in mirthful Converfe, fweetly flows,
Till gentle Sleep invites us to Repofe

The Morning come, we to the Wharfs repair,
Survey the mighty Magazines of War .
Tremendous Rows of Cannon meet our Eyes;
And Iron Deaths, in maffy Mountains rife
Store-houfe of MARS! where, rang'd in Order, lay
Ten thoufand Thunders for fome fatal Day.

Departing hence, the Dock we travel round,
Where lab'iing Shipwrights rattling Axes found·
Some bend the ftubborn Planks, while others rear
The lofty Maft, or crooked Timber fquare ,
Some ply their Engines, fome direct the Toil,
And carefully infpect the mighty Pile ;
See ev'ry Chink fecurely ftopt, before
The winged Caftle ventures from the Shore.

So, when the youthful Crane intends to fly
Her firft long Journey thro' the fpacious Sky ,
Before fhe rears herfelf fublime in Air,
She ranges ev'ry Plume with prudent Care ;
Tries if her Pinions can her Flight fuftain ;
Then fprings away, and foars above the Main.

But fee! the fmoaking, fiery Forge appears,
Vulcanian Sounds furprize our lift'ning Ears·
See ! bufy Smiths around their Anvils fweat ;
Their brawny Arms the glowing Anchor beat,
Alternately the chiming Hammers fall,
And loud Notes echo thro' the footy Hall.
Such, haply, on the founding Anvil rung,
When firft the Harp melodious TUBAL ftrung:

As TUBAL CAIN the ductile Metal wrought,
And VULCAN's heav'nly Art to Mortals taught;
The Brother, pleas'd to hear his Hammers chime,
Soon harmoniz'd their Notes to proper Time:
Man's Bosom then sonorous Organ warm'd,
The softer Lyre his gloomy Sorrows charm'd;
While Tyrants Hearts unusual Pity found,
And savage Tempers soften'd with the Sound.

'Twas now the Time, when PHOEBUS' piercing
    Ray
Shot down direct, and measur'd half the Day.
A brave * Commander luckily we meet,
Who courteously invites us to the Fleet.
A Table elegantly spread we found,
And loyal Healths the Captain pushes round;
AUGUSTUS first, and all the Royal Line,
Give sweeter Flavours to the sparkling Wine;
WAGER, and NORRIS, next, who boldly reign,
In floating Castles, Monarchs of the Main.

But now again our winged Sails we spread,
Again we visit *Paulton*'s sylvan Shade;
Where, parting from my Friend, I mount my Steed,
And, o'er the Wilds of *Wellow*, urge his Speed:
Wilds, which were lately sterile, as the Coast,
Where patient CATO march'd his fainting Host!
Nor could the Swain explore a cooling Shade,
When fervid PHOEBUS burnt his glowing Head;
Till CHANDOIS bad the dreary Desart smile
With verdant Groves, and beautify'd the Soil:
He said, ten thousand Trees adorn'd the Plain,
Ten thousand Shades, delightful to the Swain.

Hence, o'er the Plains, and fruitful Fields I pass,
Full forty Miles, till *Witney* ends my Race.

---

* Captain REDDISH, Commander of the *Amelia.*

I vifit here an elegant * Divine,
In whom the Scholar, Friend, and Critic join;
Who freely judges of an Author's Thoughts,
Improves his Beauties, and corrects his Faults;
Severely kind, and candidly fevere,
Polite, as Courtiers; and, as Truth, fincere;
Who, in MINERVA's Temple, taught our Youth
The Path to Wifdom, Virtue, Honour, Truth,
Till having, with a gen'rous Mind, beftow'd
The Flow'r of all his Years in doing Good,
Fatigu'd with Labours, and with Age decay'd,
Retires, with Honour, to the rural Shade.

So, when the Prince of Rivers, fruitful *Nile*,
Has flow'd, and fatten'd all the *Memphian* Soil,
Spent all the Riches, that his Waves contain,
Back to his Banks, he draws his humid Train.

I pay my Off'rings next at PHOEBUS' Shrine,
Oxford, the Seat of all the tuneful Nine,
Forgive me, God of Verfe, who daring greet
Thy facred Temples with unhallow'd Feet!
As pious *Muffelmen* to *Mecca* roam,
Zealous to worfhip at their Prophet's Tomb;
So comes the Poet to thy rev'rend Fanes,
Invoking thee to aid his humble Strains
O! might a Spark of thy celeftial Flame
But raife my Numbers equal to my Theme,
ALFRED immortal in my Page fhould fhine;
ALFRED, the *Monarch*, *Hero*, and *Divine*.
Who, having bravely all his Foes o'erthrown,
Advanc'd thy Kingdom, and confirm'd his own,
Water'd his Realm with the *Pierian* Spring,
Recall'd the banifh'd Arts, and bad the Mufes fing.

Then

* Rev. Dr. FRIEND.

Then should my Numbers sound with * WICKHAM's
    Praise ;
Nor less should † Fox's Fame adorn my Lays,
Whose pious Care the decent Fabric rear'd,
Which kindly shelter'd the unworthy Bard ,
Nor the unworthy Bard should leave unpaid
The grateful Debt, contracted while he stay'd :
Thy Favours, chiefly, WINDER, should be known,
In lasting Numbers, tuneful as thy own.
Thee, BODLEY, would I sing ; who can refuse
A Verse to BODLEY, Patron of the Muse ?
Whose letter'd Bounty to the World declares
The treasur'd Wisdom of three thousand Years.
Nor should the Muse forget the ‡ Prelate's Fame,
Who grac'd the River with a stately Frame,
Known by the flow'ry Meads, which round it lie,
And beauteous Walks, that charm the Student's Eye ;
Where courtly ADDISON attun'd his Lays,
And rais'd his own, by singing DRYDEN's Praise.
Hail, happy Bard ! whose Genius still could shine
In ev'ry Art , for ev'ry Art was thine :
Whether thou did'st the Critic's Pen engage,
The Critic's Pen improv'd the Poet's Rage ;
Whether thou did'st the Hero's Deeds rehearse,
The Hero's Deeds shone brighter in thy Verse :
Or did thy tragic Muse sublimely tell,
How stubborn CATO for his Country fell ;
Parties no more retain'd their factious Hate ;
All pity'd CÆSAR's, honour'd CATO's Fate :
Nor less thy soft diurnal Essays please,
That Glass, where ev'ry Fool his Folly sees ;

      K 3   Where

---

* Founder of *New* College.
† Founder of *Corpus Christi* College, where the Author was kindly entertain'd.
‡ WAINFLET, Bishop of *Winchester*, Founder of *Magdalen* College, where Mr ADDISON writ a Panegyric on Mr, DRYDEN, the first *English* Verses he ever made public.

Where Virtue fhines with fuch attractive Grace,
She tempts the Vicious to her chafte Embrace.
O! may thy Labours be a Star to guide
My Thoughts and Actions o'er Life's devious Tide;
If Pride, or Paffion check my doubtful Sail,
Let thy Inftructions lend a friendly Gale,
To waft me to the peaceful, happy Shore,
Where thou, immortal Bard! art gone before;
Then thofe who grant me not a Poet's Name,
Shall own I left behind a better Fame.

An EPIGRAM.

Words are but Wind.   Tale of a Tub,

IF Words are Wind, as fome allow;
    No Promifes can bind;
Since breaking of the ftricteft Vow,
    Is only breaking Wind.

FELIX

FELIX and *CONSTANCE.*

A Poem, taken from Boccace.

To the Right Hon. the Countefs of Pomfret,

Blown on the rolling Surface of the Deep,
The mourning Maid at length reclines to Sleep;
While confcious Vifions labour in her Breaft,
And airy Spectres difcompofe her Reft.
Sometimes fhe feems upon her native Shore,
Blefs'd with the beauteous Youth, as heretofore ;
Hears him converfe, while from his tuneful Tongue
Melodious Senfe, in melting Mufic, rung :
Sometimes fhe finds, or feems at leaft to find,
His fhatter'd Veffel forc'd before the Wind,
With foaming Waves, and furious Tempefts toft,
The Maft, and broken Sails, and Sailors, loft :
Sometimes her Dream, in frightful Forms difplay'd
A Croud of Martyrs, cruel Love had made ;
Lamenting Thysbe's Shade before her ftands,
Shews her capacious Wound, and purple Hands ;
Now lyric Sappho in the Tide expires,
Now faithful Porcia eats the living Fires.
At length, awaking from her Dream, fhe hears
A *Latian* Voice, which thus falutes her Ears .

Unhappy *Chriftian* Maid ! (for fuch, at leaft,
You, by your decent Habit, feem expreft)

Say

Say whence you came, and hither how convey'd,
Expos'd to Sea, without the Seaman's Aid?

Soon as the Nymph her native Language hears,
Her frighted Soul was fill'd with Doubts and Fears:
She thought, the adverſe Wind, or refluent Main,
Had forc'd her back to *Liparis* again;
Till, ſtarting up, a ſpacious Land ſhe ſpies;
Barbarian Caves and Cots her Sight ſurprize.
She ſees a Matron on the neighb'ring Strand;
Nor knows the Matron, nor the neighb'ring Land.
O! whither, whither am I blown? ſhe cries;
What Dens and Caves appear before my Eyes?
And who inhabit 'em? or Beaſts of Prey,
Or Men, leſs kind, and crueller than they?

To whom the Matron: Fly, nor dare to truſt
The faithleſs People of this hated Coaſt:
Here Sailors oft their hapleſs Fate deplore;
Who 'ſcape the Seas, are wreck'd upon the Shore:
For, when the forceful Wind, and foaming Deep,
To this inhuman Coaſt impel the Ship,
Around the Beach the rude Barbarians ſtray,
Deſtroy the Mariners, and ſeize their Prey;
By others Death, they keep themſelves alive,
Subſiſt by Rapine, and by Ruin thrive.

Unhappy Fate! the mourning Nymph reply'd;
O! had I periſh'd in the ſafer Tide!
For much I fear, the Land I now ſurvey,
Dooms me to greater Evils, than the Sea:
And yet what greater Ills can Fate provide,
Than thus to ſeek for Death, and be deny'd?
Not ſo my FELIX 'ſcap'd the raging Waves,
Him NEPTUNE funk, and me unkindly faves;
Saves, only to increaſe my formei Woes,
To fall, perhaps, by more ungen'rous Foes,

Or

Or to indulge some lustful Tyrant's Will.
But, O ye Heav'ns! avert the fatal Ill;
Protect my Honour in this foreign Coast,
The only Blessing which I have not lost!

The list'ning Matron wonders with Surprize,
Nor hears, unmov'd, the weeping Damsel's Cries:
But leads her to her neighb'ring Cottage, where
She chears her fainting Soul with homely Fare,
Condoles her Grief, and begs her to disclose
Her Country, Cares, and Cause of all her Woes.
Excited by her Words, the pensive Maid
Preludes with Sighs, and thus, reluctant, said.

O hospitable Dame! why would you move
A Wretch to tell a Tale of hapless Love?
Which, in relating, must renew my Grief;
Nor can I hope, nor you bestow Relief
Yet, since you seem a Partner of my Care,
'Tis just a Partner know the Weight I bear.

Not far from *Ætna's* flaming Mount I came,
From *Liparis*, and CONSTANCE is my Name:
Great Honours and Estates my Sire possess'd,
And, O! too much to make his Daughter bless'd.
I once with Fame and Fortune was supply'd,
Nor envy'd Empresses their Pomp and Pride;
Now, like a Meteor, fallen from its Height,
My Glory's vanish'd, and extinct my Light——
Full twenty Years in Happiness I pass'd,
And ev'ry Year was happier than the last.
Young FELIX then his Love began to show;
(Young FELIX was the Cause of all my Woe)
A beauteous Youth, endow'd with manly Grace;
But far his noble Soul excell'd his Face
And, tho' his niggar'd Fate had Wealth deny'd,
The Want of Wealth by Virtue was supply'd.

To

Two *Years* to win my doubtful Heart he ſtrove,
Two *Years* my doubtful Heart declin'd his Love:
Yet ſtill he preſs'd me with his am'rous Tale,
Nor found at length, 'twas fruitleſs to aſſail.
For, by Degrees, inſenſibly I came
To firſt approve, and then indulge, his Flame,
Nor could his Suit, nor would his Vows reprove,
I heard with Joy, nor thought it Sin to love,
Till in my Breaſt imperious CUPID reign'd.
Alas! how eaſy *Love* a Conqueſt gain'd!
And now my Reaſon check'd my Will no more,
But fed the Flame, it ſtrove to quench before
Yet durſt not an immodeſt Thought approve;
Love rul'd my *Heart*, but *Honour* rul'd my *Love*.
I ſcorn'd to ſtain my Virtue with a King;
As much my Lover ſcorn'd ſo mean a Thing.
What could we do? What cannot *Love* inſpire?
The Youth reveals his Paſſion to my Sire,
And in ſuch melting Accents made it known,
As might have mov'd all Fathers, but my own.
But proudly he my Lover's Suit repell'd;
And, frowning, thus our mutual Ruin ſeal'd:

No more, preſumptuous Youth! thy Paſſion name;
Suppreſs the Sparks, before they riſe to Flame.
How dar'ſt thou, vulgar Wretch, ignobly born,
My Daughter's Scandal, and her Father's Scorn!
Aſpire to wed ſo far above thy Fate?
He ſternly ſaid, and forc'd him from his Gate.

O *Avarice!* what Evils doſt thou cauſe,
Breaking the Bands of Love, and Nature's Laws?
Go, hungry God! and rule the narrow-ſoul'd;
Collect, and guard their curſt bewitching Gold;
Fit Province for thy Reign! too mean to pove
The Charms of Nuptial Life, and Joys of Love!
Ah!

Ah! what avails to gain a pompous Name,
With boasted Titles of paternal Fame,
Deriv'd from Ancestors of noble Blood?
Things common to the Vicious and the Proud!
Refulgent Equipage, and gaudy Shows,
Fictitious Ornaments of real Woes!
If Love be absent, Pomp and worldly Gain
But gild our Cares, and varnish o'er our Pain.
O! had my cruel Father thought like me,
I ne'er had prov'd the Dangers of the Sea,
Nor ever wander'd here a banish'd Maid;
And, O dear FELIX! thou hadst not been dead!

So speaks the trembling Nymph; and while she
    speaks,
The pearly Torrents stream adown her Cheeks;
Cold clammy sweats, and throbbing Sighs arise,
Slow moves the Blood, and dizzy roll her Eyes;
So much affected with her Lover's Fate,
See struggled, groan'd, and fainted from her Seat.
Her Hostess straight a grateful Cordial sought,
And to her Lips applies the chearful Draught,
Washing her Temples with reviving Oil,
The vital Spirits answer to her Toil;
The purple Tide begins to roll again,
Again diffuses Life thro' ev'ry Vein·
And now she sighing, rais'd her drooping Head;
And, Is my Death, she cries, again delay'd?
Why did you check me on the Brink of Fate?
Better the Soul had fled her loathsome Seat.
Death is the only Good I wish to know,
End of my Pain, and Period of my Woe.

To whom replies the Dame: Unhappy Fair!
Rely on Heav'n, nor let your Soul despair·
Teach me to give your troubled Heart Relief;
Or teach me how, at least, to share your Grief:
                                        Your

Your mournful Story much affects my Mind,
Yet fomething feems remaining ftill behind.

O ! much, CONSTANTIA fays, remains to come,
The fatal Part that finifhes my Doom :
For, when my FELIX, (FELIX now no more !)
Was banifh'd from my haughty Father's Door,
Not able to obtain me for his Bride,
Nor willing to refign me, tho' deny'd ;
Hope, from Defpair, his daring Soul conceives :
A Bark he builds, to plough the briny Waves :
Then call'd a few Domeftics to his Aid,
Embrac'd me in his Arms, and fighing, faid :

O Thou, for ever dear, for ever bleft,
At once the Joy, and Trouble of my Breaft !
Since Poverty expels me from thy Arms,
Since Wealth alone is worthy of thy Charms;
I fwear by all the mighty Pow'rs above,
(Sad Fate that drives me from the Nymph I love !)
To try my Fortune on remoter Shores,
And feek the Gold, thy Sire fo much adores.
Perhaps the Planets, unpropitious here,
In other Climes may kinder Afpects wear ,
May lead me where the rocky Di'monds lie,
Or where the golden Mines may Wealth fupply ;
If not, the laft fad Pleafure is to die.

Such was the fatal Vow he rafhly made ;
A fatal Vow, and fatally obey'd !
Struck dumb, my Tears the Want of Words fupply'd;
His, mixt with mine, increas'd the pearly Tide.
Yet, left I fhould his Refolution fhake,
He rufh'd away, and mounted on the Deck :
His hafty Crew expand the fwelling Sails,
Strong rolls the Sea before impulfive Gales ;

The

The crooked Keel the frothy Flood divides,
Swift flies the Ship, and rushes thro' the Tides.

My Lover long my gazing Eyes pursue;
As long my Lover kept me in his View.
Reluctant so, departing Souls prepare,
To wing their doubtful Flight, they know not where;
Reluctant so, expiring Bodies lie,
Nor willing these to stay, nor those to fly.

Twice twenty Days I spent in fruitless Tears,
Before the fatal Tidings reach'd my Ears,
How FELIX failing o'er the watry Way,
Was wreck'd on Rocks, and perish'd in the Sea.
O! then what Trouble, Grief, and anxious Care,
Confus'd my Soul, and bent it to Despair!
I curs'd the Cause, that forc'd him to expire;
O Heav'n! forgive me, if I curs'd my Sire:
I fled his House, and sought the lonely Grove,
(The gloomy Witness of my former *Love.*)
Where, once resolv'd to seek the Shades below,
I drew the Knife, to strike the mortal Blow;
Till Piety the cruel Thought suppreſt,
And check'd the *Roman* Courage of my Breaſt:
Trembling saw two doubtful Paths, nor knew,
Which Path was best to shun, or which pursue;
Oppoſing Paſſions in my Bosom ſtrove,
And *Conscience* now prevail'd, and now my *Love.*

As when the Wind and Tide a Conteſt make,
The Sailor, trembling, sees his Veſſel ſhake,
This Way, and that, and both, by Turns reclin'd,
As swells the Surge, or blows the furious Wind.
So was my Soul with diff'rent Notions sway'd,
Of this, of that, of both, and all afraid
Ah! why should Mortals of their *Reason* boaſt,
Which moſt deſerts 'em, when they want it moſt?

L   For,

For, when the troubled Mind's confus'd with Pain,
'Tis but an *Ignis Fatuus* of the Brain;
Which, if our wand'ring Souls from *Virtue* ſtray,
But leads us more and more from *Virtue's* Way:
So led it me to ſtem the devious Tide,
And ſeek for Death, where wretched FELIX dy'd.

Not diſtant far, a fiſhing Veſſel ſtood,
Nor wholly on the Land, nor in the Flood ·
Arriv'd to this, I row'd it from the Shore,
And, bent on Death, the Tide I now explore;
Expecting, ſoon, the friendly-furious Wave
Would give my Troubles and myſelf a Grave.
But, when I ſaw the Billows round me flow,
The boundleſs Skies above, and Seas below,
Scar'd with the Terrors of the watry Space,
I wrapt my Mantle round my tim'rous Face
Then lay me down, to all the Dangers blind,
Chance was my *Compaſs*, and my *Pilot*, *Wind*
Blown here and there, I floated on the Deep,
Which rock'd my Eyes, but not my Fears aſleep
For now my dreaming Soul, in Fancy's Maze,
A thouſand tragic airy Ghoſts ſurveys,
Which flutter'd round me, and reproaching, ſaid,
Die, Coward! follow FELIX to the Shade.
Why wouldſt thou wiſh to live, now he is dead?
But when, at length, your friendly Voice I heard,
My Viſion ceas'd, the Spectres diſappear'd.
Thus have I told, but can't diſpel my Care,
For who can conquer *Love*, or cure *Deſpair?*

Thus ſhe; and thus CAPRESA ſpake again:
(So was ſhe call'd who wak'd her on the Main)
Unhappy Nymph! compoſe your troubled Mind,
Nor doubt the gracious Guide of human Kind:
That GOD, who ſav'd you from the foamy Wave,
Will doubtleſs guard the Life, he deign'd to ſave.

Vouch

Vouchsafe to take the Counsel I can lend ·
At *Suja* Heav'n has bless'd me with a Friend,
Much fam'd for Wealth, for pious Actions more ;
No Husband, and no Children, but the Poor.
Let me conduct you to her friendly Gate ;
(Too small my Cottage for a Guest so great)
She will protect ye from Barbarian Foes,
With prudent Counsel mitigate your Woes,
And charm your ruffled Soul to soft Repose.

Blest Partner of my Grief ! the Damsel said,
Some Angel surely sent you to my Aid,
For now some dawning Rays of Hope appear,
That chace away the Clouds of dark despair.
This Pause of Pain, and Interval of Grace,
Shall be employ'd in Search of future Peace.
Then guide and guard me to your noble Friend,
So may you never want this Aid you lend !
And, as we travel, deign to let me know,
To whom so many Thanks I justly owe ;
What hapless Fortune cast you on this Land,
What Occupation here employs your Hand.
Sweet Conversation may suspend my Care,
Dispel my Grief, or make it less severe
So shall I easier reach the neighb'ring Town ;
And, list'ning to your Fate, forget my own.

Thus she ; and thus the pensive Dame replies ·
(With briny Drops distilling from her Eyes)
Fain would I, lovely Nymph ! suspend your Care,
Dispel your Grief, or make it less severe :
But, were I all my Fortune to explain,
'Twould not alleviate, but increase your Pain ;
For in your Soul such Sparks of Nature glow,
As make you share your Neighbour's Joy or Woe.
The *Christian* Faith I secretly embrace,
Tho' doom'd to dwell among a *Pagan* Race ·

Treparum wasted all my Bloom of Life,
Where long I liv'd, a Farmer's happy Wife:
My careful, loving Husband till'd the Soil,
Nor was the Field ungrateful to his Toil.
For, ev'ry *Summer*, CERES crown'd the Plain;
Each *Autumn* fill'd the Barn with golden Grain:
So thick the verdant Harvest yearly stood,
The Meadows seem'd to groan beneath their Load,
Our fleecy Flocks were fruitful of their Young,
Hail were our Oxen, and our Horses strong,
Nor did our Kine of milky Produce fail,
But with distended Udders fill'd the Pail
'Twas then, alas! how often have I cry'd,
I would not wish to be a Monarch's Bride!
When all around my little Infants came,
Hung on my Knees, and lisp'd their *Mama*'s Name,
Or met their Father with the Ev'ning Ray,
Embrac'd his Neck, and kiss'd his Cares away.
Soon as their riper Age cou'd Labour bear,
We sent 'em forth to feed the fleecy Care,
Where often have we spent the *Summer*'s Day,
Charm'd to behold the wanton Cattle's Play.
What Pleasure twas to see the skipping Lambs?
What Music, when they bleated for their Dams?
We thought our Joys could never be increas'd,
Love, Peace, and Plenty join'd to make us bless'd.
But see how *Fortune* holds her fickle Reign!
She raises up to tumble down again.
For now our Thread of Happiness was spun;
The Gains of twenty Years were lost in one.
'Twas in the Season, when the verdant Mead
Begins to ask the Mower's crooked Blade;
Before the Wheat receives a yellow Stain,
Or milky Juice is harden'd into Grain;
A Gale of Poison baleful EURUS cast,
The vernal Product sicken'd with the Blast;

Our

Our Meadows ſtraight a Saffron Scene diſcloſe,
Our infant Apples quit the blighted Boughs,
Peaſe, Wheat, and Barley, wither'd in the Fields,
And Nature one abortive Harveſt yields
Nor ſtopt it here, the flying Plague began
To ſpread the bane in Beaſts, and thence to Man:
Firſt dy'd our Sheep upon the ruſſet Plain,
Next ſwell'd our Oxen with a fatal Blain;
Here tumbles o'er her Meat, the moping Cow;
There drops the panting Horſe before the Plough:
At length the dire Contagion ſpread ſo wide,
My Virgin Children made the Tomb their Bride.
This Nature bore——But when our Landlord ſent
His Officers, to ſeize my Lord for Rent;
And he, to ſhun the Priſon, flies the Shore;
Liſts on the Sea, to tug the lab'ring Oar?
I wept, I rav'd, I curs'd the baleful Air;
And fled my native Land, but not my Care.
Thus, baniſh'd here, a Widow, and a Wife,
Condemn'd to ſuffer not enjoy a Life,
I toil for thoſe, who catch the finny Prey;
The Toils are great, but very ſmall the Pay!
Their ſcaly Fry to Market oft I bear,
Oft in the Ocean waſh their thready Snare;
And then was waſhing, when, with great Surprize,
You, and your floating Veſſel, met my Eyes.

Now Heav'n defend us both! the Nymph reply'd;
And can ſuch Rage in *Chriſtian* Minds reſide?
What, could the curſt, inhuman Tyrant wreſt
Thy tender Huſband from thy loving Breaſt,
When all thy Wealth was loſt, thy Children dead?
O *Virtue! Virtue!* whither art thou fled?
Why muſt ſuch Evils on the Guiltleſs flow?
Ye Heav'ns! is Innocence rewarded ſo?

So fpake the Nymph; her Friend no more replies;
For now PRISCILLA's Dome attracts their Eyes:
Approaching to her friendly Gate, they found
The gen'rous Lady dealing Alms around
To needy Souls, a haplefs, helplefs Crowd,
Who daily blefs'd her Hand for daily Food !
When thus CAPRESA. Hail, for ever blefs'd !
'Tis Godlike thus to fuccour the Diftrefs'd.
Yet none of thefe, who claim your *Chriftian* Aid,
Deferves it more than this unhappy Maid,
Who once was blefs'd with Fame and Riches too,
Tho' fickle Fortune now is turn'd her Foe,
Unlike the Mendicants, who daily fhare
Your friendly Bounty, and paternal Care.

To whom the Lady, with a gracious Look,
That feem'd to breathe Compaffion, while fhe fpoke:
Sure Decency forbids, a Gueft fo great
Should, undiftinguifh'd, with the Vulgar eat.
No, deck my Table with the choiceft Fare,
The Nymph, with me, a kind Repaft fhall fhare,
For, by her Looks, if Truth may be divin'd,
That lovely Body cloaths a lovely Mind.

She faid, and CONSTANCE low Obeifance made,
Then gladly follow'd, where PRISCILLA led.
Within the Gate a fpacious Room fhe found,
Whofe Walls were beautify'd with Tap'ftry round
Where pious Tales appear'd, fo lively wrought,
The Work feem'd vital, and the Figures Thought:
Here, in the Shade, the *Jewifh* Patriarch ftood,
Feafting the Sons of Heav'n with earthly Food;
While, there, the good *Samaritan* confeft
His Kindnefs, and reproach'd the cruel *Prieft*;
With many more, a charitable Band,
The fkilful Labour of PRISCILLA's Hand.

Hither

Hither the Dame convey'd a sweet Repaft ?
Rich Meats, and rofy Wines the Tables grac'd :
They eat, they drank, in pleafing Converfe join'd ;
And chear'd at once the Body and the Mind.
The Call of Nature being foon fuppreft,
Thus fpake the Lady to her youthful Gueft.

Say, lovely Stranger ! (for I long to know;
So may propitious Heav'n remove thy Woe !)
Whence thus reduc'd ? By Famine, Sword, or Fire ?
What Sire thy Beauty boafts, what Land thy Sire ?
Perhaps fome Princefs, banifh'd from her Home,
Thus condefcends to grace my ruftic Dome .
If fo, I greatly fear, my homely Feaft
Has been unworthy of my Royal Gueft.

She faid, the Nymph unfolds her Tale again ;
The prudent Dame attempts to foothe her Pain,
And thus reply'd . Tho' weighty are your Woes,
The weightieft Ill, with Patience, lighter grows :
Then bear with Patience all that Heav'n defign'd,
Whofe Ways are juft, though difficult to find,
Plann'd for the gen'ral Good of human Kind.
God's Paths in winding Mazes often lie,
Too intricate for feeble Reafon's Eye ;
Moft regular, when in Confufion loft ,
Moft conftant, when they feem to vary moft.
Perhaps his Mercy forc'd you thus to roam,
To fhun a more unhappy Fate at home ,
For with one Evil he removes a worfe,
And bleffes oft with what we think a Curfe.
Then let your Soul at Fortune not repine ,
But truft in Heav'n's Protection, next, in mine:
In me you ftill fhall find a faithful Friend,
With whom, in Time, your Troubles all may end:
But, fince you now are harrafs'd out with Woes,
Refiefh your weary Soul with fweet Repofe,

And

And when you wake, at Morning, may you find
Heav'n's balmy Comfort heal your wounded Mind!

Thus chear'd, the Nymph obfequioufly withdrew,
And bath'd her Cares in Sleep's refreshing Dew,
Till PHOEBUS, rifing from the Shades of Night,
With rofy Keys unlock'd the Gates of Light
Bright as his Beams, arofe the beauteous Maid;
And, to her Patronnefs returning, faid:

What Thanks, propitious Lady! fhall I give
For all the Godlike Bounties I receive?
O! let my *Silence* thank you; for I know,
Words can't exprefs the Gratitude I owe.

To whom replies the venerable Dame.
No other Thanks, but Gratitude I claim:
The Terms of Charity are never hard,
Love and Compaffion are their own Reward:
A Soul, that fuccours Virtue, when diftreft,
Can with Reflection make a noble Feaft,
Which nourifhes the Mind, and overpays
A gen'rous Deed with felf-approving Praife.

Such was their Converfe, till domeftic Care
Invites PRISCILLA from the youthful Fair;
Who fat in penfive Solitude, and ftrove
To foften, or fufpend the Pains of Love.
At length the Linen on her Knee fhe fpread,
And with her Needle mark'd the docile Thread.
Young THYSBE's Fate fhe firft began to frame,
But foon commits her Labour to the Flame:
Next drew fhe HERO finking in the Main,
Then raz'd the finifh'd Image out again,
Both thefe difpleas'd her, tho' judicious Art,
And Rays of Nature fhone in ev'ry Part.

At

At length her own unhappy Tale she chose,
And lively paints the Scene of all her Woes:
Her charming FELIX first the Linen grac'd,
By whom her Father, frowning stern she plac'd:
Her Lover's Parting next to these appears;
(But, weeping here, she foil'd her Work with Tears)
Next, on the Seas, she drew his floating Ship,
Next, her own Boat, slow-wand'ring on the Deep:
By these she fix'd CAPRESA on the Strand,
Who wak'd her first, and welcom'd her to Land:
The good PRISCILLA last employ'd her Art,
Whose Aspect spoke the Bounty of her Heart;
Her friendly Roof, a Refuge for the Poor,
The Horn of Plenty, pendent o'er the Door,
Diffusing Blessings still, and still increasing more.
All these confest such Beauty, Skill, and Care,
Not HELEN better wove the *Trojan* War,
While HECTOR, PARIS, and their Martial Train,
With *Grecian* Heroes battled on the Plain,

Here let us leave the lovely Nymph a while,
To pass her tedious Hours in pleasing Toil,
Her absent Lover now my Song pursues,
Whose valiant Deeds require a nobler Muse.

Swift-pinion'd FAME, which often babbling flies,
To bear the unwelcome Truths, and oftner Lies,
Had spread the ductile Error far and wide,
How wand'ring FELIX perish'd in the Tide.
But FELIX safely reach'd the *Thunic* Port,
And soon arriv'd to Honours in the Court·
His Wisdom there the wisest Peers excell'd;
His Valour more surpass'd 'em in the Field.
When first he to the Royal Palace came,
An Accident occur'd to raise his Fame:
A noble Lord there was, of great Renown,
Rebell'd against the King and claim'd his Crown;
Great

Great Preparations made he for the Fight;
Nor lefs the Monarch to defend his Right;
But fummon'd all to meet the daring Foe,
Whofe Strength could wield a Sword or bend a Bow,
And promis'd to reward their Martial Care,
With Honours equal to their Deeds in War.

Now rings the Region with the Foe's Alarms,
Terrific fhines the Field with burnifh'd Arms,
The Martial Trumpet, founding from afar,
With dreadful Notes, proclaims approaching War.
The Royal Army valiant FELIX join'd,
Intrepid Courage animates his Mind.
Fix'd in the Front, the Foe he bravely dares,
Like PALLAS prudent, and as bold as MARS
Say, Mufe, what Goddefs, that tremendous Hour,
Aided the Youth with fuch unufual Pow'r?
Bright VENUS, confcious of the Lover's Smart,
Sharpen'd his Sword, and pointed ev'ry Dart.
Fierce, as a Lion, thro' the Lines he fprung,
And forc'd his Foes, like trembling Stags along.

As when refiftlefs Winds rufh o'er the Deep,
And from its Anchor force the driving Ship,
Or furioufly againft the Woodland roar,
The leafy Harveft, tumbling, flies before:
So rufh'd the Hero on the adverfe Band,
So fled the Legions from his pow'rful Hand;
Till foon the Rebel Lord he Pris'ner made,
And to the King his captive Prize convey'd.

Now reaps the Youth the Glory of his Toil;
To him the Monarch gives the Martial Spoil,
Rewards his Valour with a noble Poft,
And makes him firft Commander of his Hoft.
Thus, quickly FELIX gain'd a deathlefs Name;
Thus, was his Labour crown'd with Wealth and Fame,

But

But Wealth and Fame infipid Things appear;
To give them Tafte, he wants the lovely Fair;
The lovely Fair, oppreft with equal Grief,
To make her happy, wants the glorious Chief.

His Fame, which foon at *Sufa* was reveal'd,
(Heroic Actions feldom he conceal'd)
With pleafing Wonder ftruck CONSTANTIA's Ears,
And fill'd her doubtful Soul with Hopes and Fears,
For, tho' the wife PRISCILLA often ftrove
With prudent Counfel to fupprefs her Love;
Her Love was only leffen'd, not fuppreft,
But glows again, again diftracts her Breaft.

As when, in rural Cots, the Flames afpire,
And lab'ring Peafants quench the mounting Fire
If Chance a latent Spark remain behind,
In heapy Afhes, fann'd with ambient Wind;
The Fires again, with former Fury, rife,
Flame thro' the Roof, and flafh into the Skies:
So in her Bofom glows the am'rous Fire
And fills her tender Soul with foft Defire.
And is my FELIX yet alive? fhe fays,
And is he crown'd with Wealth, and deathlefs Praife?
No, no, I fear the flatt'ring Tale deceives;
Methinks I fee him plunging in the Waves.
Ah! why, ye Heav'ns, are feeble Mortals curft,
In Things uncertain, to believe the Worft?
No; rather let me fee the *Thanic* Court;
There, with my Eyes, confirm the bleft Report:
Hope flies before, and points the pleafing Way,
Love urges on, and *Love* I muft obey.

So faying, to PRISCILLA ftraight fhe came,
And with her Thoughts acquaints the pious Dame;
The pious Dame, with tender Pity fway'd,
Approves the Paffion of the loving Maid,

And,

And, with CAPRESA, guards her to the Place,
Refolv'd herfelf to view the Hero's Face,
The Hero meets them at the Regal Gate,
Array'd in Armour formidably great,
For on that Morning, by the King's Command,
The Chief was to review the Martial Band:
His ftudded Chariot darted Splendor round,
His ftately Courfers, neighing, paw'd the Ground;
The nodding Plumes around his Temples wave,
With awful Grace, and beautifully brave.
He knew th'approaching Nymph, but, in Surprize,
The joyous Stream defcended from his Eyes
The Nymph beheld the weeping Chief, nor knew,
For what he wept, nor whom fhe came to view:
His Martial Drefs, befpangled o'er with Gold,
The dreadful *Warrior*, not the *Lover*, told
But, when he caft the Helmet from his Head,
And thro' the Gates the blufhing Damfel led;
She knew her Lover, clafp'd him to her Breaft,
While filent Eloquence her Joy confeft.
The confcious Pains an abfent Lover bears,
Defpair, fallacious *Hope*, and anxious *Fears*,
For Want of Words, were painted with their Tears
And when, at length, their chryftal Sluices ceas'd,
The joyful Hero thus the Nymph addrefs'd:

Ye Gods! and have I then my Charmer found.
And are my Labours thus compleatly crown'd!
Yes! let me clafp thee to my longing Arms,
Drink in thy Breath, and feed upon thy Charms,
As widow'd Turtles, roving round the Fields,
Thro' all the fruitful Stores, which Nature yields,
Curft in the midft of Plenty, cannot eat,
But ftarve, lamenting for their abfent Mate
Thus have I been with Fame and Riches grac'd;
Yet wanted thee to give my Riches Tafte.

But

But say, how came this Wealth I wanted most?
What brought my *Love* to this Barbarian Coast?

He said; and now the joyful Damsel spake,
The Dangers which she suffer'd for his sake;
Shews him the Dame, who found her on the Tide;
PRISCILLA too, who all her Wants supply'd.
Then, prostrate, on her Knees before him bends,
And begs him to reword her faithful Friends.
The grateful Chief, by native Goodness sway'd,
Embrac'd 'em both, and soon the Nymph obey'd;
But first before his royal Master came,
And begs he may resign his Post of Fame.
At which the Monarch frowns with awful Eyes;
Till FELIX straight, who saw his Passion rise,
Falls on the Ground, and to his Master shews
The various Scene of all his am'rous Woes.
This heard, the King resumes his former Grace;
Love tun'd his Soul, and smooth'd his ruffled Face:
He rais'd the Hero, bids the Nymph appear;
The Nymph approach'd him with a modest Fear;
Before his awful Throne, submiss, she fell,
And to him straight unfolds th'amazing Tale.
Mute, on the Ground, a-while he fix'd his Eyes;
Then, Is the Force of Love so great? he cries.
We falsely *Man* the World's Commander call,
Thou, mightier Monarch, *Love!* commandest All·
Young AMMON's Self could not thy Pow'r confine;
The *World his* Subject was, but *He was thine.*

Then, smiling, thus he chear'd the trembling Fair,
Henceforward, lovely Nymph, dismiss thy Care,
For, since thy Love has conquer'd Wind and Sea,
Curst be the King, that's crueller than they!
Let HYMEN straight confirm the Marriage Ties;
Thou justly hast deserv'd the Nuptial Prize.

M   This

This faid, he crown'd the Hero's Martial Care
With Riches far fuperior to the Fair:
Due Thanks return'd, they to PRISCILLA came,
Beftowing Gifts and Honours on the Dame.
CAPRESA next, with Age and Labour worn,
In comely Robes the grateful Pair adorn;
With ample Wealth her former Blifs reftor'd,
And from the Seas redeem'd her Nuptial Lord;
Her Nuptial Lord again enjoys his Wife,
Again del ¸htful Freedom crowns his Life;
Till *Nature* calls him to refign his Breath,
In honourable Age, and peaceful Death.

This done, the loving Couple quit the Shore,
And joyfully the deftin'd Port explore;
While fportive NEREIDS round their Veffel play,
And wanton CUPIDS hail them on their Way;
Rough THETIS' Self affumes a pleafing Smile,
Glad to return them to their native Soil;
Where facred HYMEN join'd their mutual Hands,
And Heav'n, indulgent, blefs'd their Nuptial Bands.

An

An Imitation of the TENTH ODE *of the*
SECOND *Book of* HORACE.

Rectus vives, LICINI, *neque altum.*
Semper urgendo, &c.

To the Right Honourable the Lord Vifcount
PALMERSTON.

IF we, my Lord, with eafy Strife,
  Would pafs this fickle Tide of Life;
We muft not always rafhly fail
With ev'ry light inconftant Gale;
Nor yet, at ev'ry Surge that roars,
Too tim'rous feek the craggy Shores.
The Man who keeps the *Golden Mean,*
Where raging Storms are feldom feen,
Avoids the dang'rous Rocks and Pools,
That fright the Wife, and fwallow Fools:
He's ne'er defpis'd among the Crowd,
  Nor envy'd in the Court,
But fteers between the Bafe and Proud,
  To gain the peaceful Port.

While lofty Spires and Cedars fall,
  Storm-beaten, to the Plain,
The lowly Shrub, and humble Wall,
  Are Proof to Wind and Rain;

And

And Lightnings guiltlefs o'er the Cottage fly;
But fmite th'ambitious Hills, that, tow'ring, threat the
    Sky.

    The fteady Mind, that's truly great,
    Surveys, unmov'd, the Turns of Fate:
    If Wealth and Fame his Pride increafe,
      His Fears their Force controul,
    If adverfe Fortune would deprefs,
      Hope elevates his Soul,
    Becaufe he knows the Pow'r who brings
    The *Winter* with its dreary Wings,
    Can make the vernal Beauties grow,
And turn our Woe to Blifs, or Blifs to Woe.
    If now on anxious Cares you feed,
    A Feaft of Joy may foon fucceed.
      To chear your penfive Mind.
    With Times, our Tempers vary round;
    Nothing immutable is found,
      But all to Change inclin'd.
    Tho' POPE with Illnefs oft complains,
    POPE is not always rack'd with Pains,
      But, warm'd with PHOEBUS' Fire,
    Sometimes he wakes the fleeping String,
    Or bids the filent Mufes fing,
      And charms us with his Lyre.

    Our Life's at beft, a chequer'd Scene,
    Of Health and Sicknefs, Mirth and Spleen:
    Yet, fince we all muft ftem this Sea,
      Where Calm and Tempeft dwell;
    Grieve not to fteer the deftin'd Way,
      But ftrive to pafs it well:
    If adverfe Storms begin to rave,
    Serenely view the foaming Wave,
Collected in yourfelf, and refolutely brave.

Or,

Or, if you find indulgent Gales
   Impel the Bark too faft,
Wifely contract the fwelling Sails,
   And check their rapid Hafte;
Left, in your fwift Career, the Ship
Split on a Rock, and fink beneath the Deep.

An IMITATION

Of the SIXTEENTH ODE

Of the SECOND Book of HORACE.

Otium Divos rogat in patenti
Prenfus Ægeo, &c.

I.

THE trembling Merchant begs for Eafe,
   When toft upon the foaming Seas;
When frowning Clouds obfcure the Skies,
And dreadful Thunder roars, and Lightning flies.

II.

For Eafe the proud *Iberians* pray,
When Martial Engines round 'em play;
The mighty *Turk* and *Perfian* too,
Beg Heav'n for Eafe, which Riches can't beftow.

M 3   III.

III.

Not filver Mines, or fhining Gold,
Nor all the Gems the *Indies* hold,
Nor purple Robes, nor pompous State,
Can cure the flutt'ring Cares which vex the Great,

IV.

Happy the Man, whofe frugal Board
Supplies the Wifhes of its Lord;
No fears torment his quiet Breaft,
No fordid Av'rice breaks his grateful Reft.

V.

Why fhould we fo much Wealth defire,
When Life fo little will require?
Why fhould we rove from Zone to Zone,
And for another Climate change our own?

VI.

Not thofe, who fly from Pole to Pole,
Can fly the Cares, which rack the Soul;
But, in remoteft Regions, find,
They leave their Country, not themfelves, behind.

VII.

For, tho' we crofs the briny Deep,
Corroding Care purfues the Ship;
It hunts the Horfeman clofe behind,
More fwift than Mountain Roes, or rapid Wind.

VIII.

The Man, contented with his State,
Anticipates no evil Fate;
Tho' Fortune is inconftant ftill,
With what is good, he fweetens what is ill.

IX,

IX

The Draught of Life is mixt, at beft;
There's none can be completely bleft
Some overlive their Pleafures here;
Some die, before they tafte what Pleafures are.

X.

Age, Wars, and Tumults, factious Hate,
Made * COTTINGTON defire his Fate;
While tender † SHEFFIELD meets his Doom
Juft in the Flow'r of Life, and youthful Bloom.

XI.

All make their *Exit* foon or late;
And, if the Gods contract thy Date,
The vital Hour, deny'd to thee,
Their more indulgent Hand may give to me.

XII.

What tho' thy fruitful Paftures keep
A hundred Flocks of bleating Sheep ?
What tho' thy proud, exulting Mares
Neigh, foam, and fly before thy gilded Cars ?

XIII.

Thy Board tho' twenty Difhes grace ?
Thy Coat as many Yards of Lace ?
I envy not the purple Dye,
Nor all thy gaudy Pomp of Luxury.

XIV.

I fhare fome Sparks of PHOEBUS' Fire,
To warm my Breaft, if not infpire,
Too little Wealth to make me proud,
And Senfe enough to fcorn the envious Crowd.

An

* See CLARENDON's Hiftory, *Lib.* 13.
† Late Duke of *Buckingham.*

An IMITATION

Of the SIXTEENTH ODE

Of the THIRD Book of HORACE.

Inclusam DANAEN *turris ahenea,*
Robustæque fores, &c.

To the Reverend Mr. STANLEY.

BELIEVE me, Sir, your Coft and Cares,
Your Dogs and Locks, your Bolts and Bars,
Your Pallifades, and Walls of Brafs,
Are all too weak, when Gold attacks the Place.
A brazen Tow'r ACRISIUS rear'd;
A brazen Tow'r, he thought, would guard
His Daughter from the leach'rous Arms
Of thofe who nightly fought her Charms;
While furly Maftiffs watch'd the Dame,
And thund'ring told if Lovers came·
Thefe kept the Nymph from Gods and Men,
Not JOVE himfelf could enter in,
Till VENUS (wondrous to behold!)
Transform'd his Godfhip into Gold.
O STANLEY, STANLEY! Gold has Pow'r
   The fterneft Heart to move,
To burft the Wall, or pierce the Tow'r,
   Impervious ev'n to JOVE.

Gold

Gold can the subtlest Head deceive,
  Or Peace, or War can bring,
Buy Votes, raise *Gallic* Arms, and give
  The *Polanders* a King.
A P O L L O knew the Force of Gold,
When PHILLIP's Martial Fate he thus foretold:
" The sharpest Lance of Steel may err,
  " So may the surest Bow ,
" But know, O King, the *Golden* Spear
  " Will vanquish ev'ry Foe."
The God's Advice the Prince pursu'd;
He fought with Gold, and Gold subdu'd;
Whence some Historians say, 'twas *this.*
And not young AMMON's Father, conquer'd *Greece.*
Gold has an absolute Command,
  It rules at Sea, as well as Land :
For, when two adverse Fleets engage,
And fiery Tubes displode their Rage;
A Bribe can make their Thunder cease,
And hush the watry World to Peace.
Yet, notwithstanding all its Force,
It often brings the greatest Curse:
Vexatious Cares and Discontents
  Increasing Gold attend,
Desires enlarge, as Wealth augments,
  For Av'rice knows no End.
We labour up the golden Hill with Pain;
But ne'er surmount the tow'ring *Alps* of Gain.

O STANLEY, Honour of my Muse !
  I fear, and justly fear,
To steer the Course Ambition shews,
  Or soar beyond my Sphere.
He's poor, who always after Wealth aspires;
He's rich, who always curbes his own Desires.
I more admire an humble Seat,
Than all the Pomps, which vex the Great;

And

And from their gilded Roofs retire,
On *Isis* Banks to tune my Lyre
In this Retreat I'm nobler bless'd,
　　Then CROESUS e'er could be,
Than if (like Misers) I possess'd
　　A *wealthy Poverty*.

While favour'd by the best of Queens,
　　Who all my Wants supplies ;
While fragrant Groves, and flow'ry Scenes,
　　Delight my Muse's Eyes ;
My Fate a far superior Blessing brings,
Than all the Pageantry of *Eastern* Kings.
　　What tho' no Flocks, on *Richmond* Plain,
　　　With Fleeces deck my Pride ?
　　What tho' I seldom drink *Champagne*,
　　　Or quaff the purple Tide ?
If these I wanted, were your Bard to ask
I know, your gen'rous Soul would send a *Cask*.

I make my Wants and Wealth agree;
I pay my Debts no worse than he,
Who o'er the Seas extends his Reign,
And adds all *Sicily* to *Spain*.
Who covets most, is most in Need,
And always rides a restless Steed,
Which foams, and flies without Controul,
Still seeks, but ne'er obtains the Goal.

Then happy those, whom Heav'n has bless'd,
　　With what may Life sustain ,
Nor are with pinching Want depress'd,
　　Nor curst with too much Gain .
For boundless Wealth ne'er fills a boundless Mind;
The Man who still pursues, is still behind.

Felix,

Felix, qui patriis ævum transegit in agris,

   Ipsa domus puerum quem videt, ipsa senem, &c.

Imitated from CLAUDIAN.

I.

HOW bless'd the Swain of *Bethnal-Green*,
   Who ne'er a Court beheld,
Nor ever rov'd beyond the Scene
   Of his paternal Field!

II.

But, where he prov'd the Go-cart's Aid,
   He prov'd the Crutch's too;
One only House his Mansion made.
   Till Life (tho' late) withdrew,

III.

False Fortune ne'er, with Smile or Frown,
   Or rais'd him, or deprest;
Her Frowns's and Smiles were both unknown
   To his contented Breast.

IV.

The Chance of Stocks he never try'd,
   Nor knew to buy or sell;
So 'scap'd the dreadful golden Tide,
   Where *South-Sea* Merchants fell.

V.

V.

Skill'd in no Bufinefs but his own,
　He fhun'd the noify Bar ;
Nor ever prov'd the fmoky Town,
　But breath'd a purer Air.

VI.

Nor by *Lord Mayor's Day* he knew
　The rolling Year to bound ;
Nor kept an Almanac to fhew
　How Seafons vary'd round.

VII.

He *Summer* knew by Heat extreme,
　The *Winter* by its Cold ;
POMONA fhew'd when *Autumn* came,
　When *Spring,* gay FLORA told.

VIII.

He planted once an Acorn fmall,
　And liv'd to fee it rife
A mighty Oak, fo wond'rous tall,
　It feem'd to prop the Skies.

IX.

And, by the Shade its Branches caft,
　Could he much truer know,
What Hour, and how his Moments paft,
　Than by the Clock of *Bow.*

X

Tho' *London* ftood fo near his Cot,
　He never mark'd the *Dome* ;
But thought St. *Paul's* as far remote,
　As *Peter's* Church at *Rome.*

XI.

XI.

Of *Isis* he was only told,
  But ne'r beheld her Streams;
Nor knew, but that the *Ganges* roll'd
  Near as the neighb'ring *Thames.*

XII.

Of Jellies, Creams, Ragous, and Tarts,
  His Stomach never thought;
A perfect Stranger to the Arts
  Luxurious Cooks have taught !

XIII.

Yet, with a simple Food supply'd,
  His Health was so entire,
That when his antient Children dy'd,
  They left a youthful Sire.

XIV.

Let others search for golden Bliss
  On *India*'s wealthy Shore ;
Their Joys of Life are less than his,
  Their Labours ten times more.

Of

Of FRIENDSHIP.

To CELIA.

O CELIA! You, whose Rays of *friendly* Fire,
Conftant as thofe of Nature, ne'er expire;
If in your Breaft no weighty Cares you find,
Nor better Thoughts employ your gen'rous Mind,
Vouchfafe an Ear. Thefe Numbers are your Due;
I fing of *Friendfhip*, and I fing to *You*
Friendfhip! a Theme, which all Mankind profefs,
No Virtue more admire, none practife lefs,
For moft have learn'd the *Grecian* * Sage's Text,
" To love one Day, as if to hate the next"
They change, forfake, as ferves their felfifh Ends,
Nor are their Dreffes vary'd more than Friends.

You therefore, who are worthy Friendfhip's Name,
And cherifh in your Breaft the genuine Flame,
Attend to what a faithful Mufe imparts,
A Mufe unpractis'd in fallacious Arts
Tho' young in Life, that Life has made her know,
A friendly Afpect oft conceals a Foe,
That, tho' fo many feeming Friends abound,
For one that's true, a thoufand falfe are found.

When firft you ftrive a faithful Friend to find,
Explore the fecret Motives of his Mind;

Nor,

* BIAS in CICERO *de Amic.* § 16.

Nor, rashly credulous, his Friendship trust,
Before you know, what Passion rules him most:
But, as a Horseman checks the Courser's Speed,
Till he has try'd the Temper of his Steed,
So check the Reins of Friendship, till you prove,
What sways the Persons, Interest, or Love.

Avoid the Fop impertinently vain,
And shun the Slave, who flatters you for Gain;
Beware of him, who sells you for a Jest;
But, most of all, beware the leaky Breast:
(Who hopes to keep the Wine the Season round,
Must first be sure his Cask be sweet and sound)
Nor should a formal Fool your Friendship claim,
Tho' Wealth and Honours dignify his Name
Let Knaves and Fools in kindred Vices join,
Chuse you a Friend, where Sense and Virtue shine;
Whose Passions move by Reason's Rule alone,
Much better, if agreeing with your own.
The Hart and Lion at a Distance keep,
Wolves company with Wolves, and Sheep with Sheep;
So we, by Nature's sympathetic Pow'rs,
Most love those Tempers, that resemble ours.

Yet, if it be too difficult to find
A Friend so justly moulded to your Mind,
Among the virtuous Few select the best,
And such is he, whose Failings are the least:
Let him a modest Freedom always claim,
To praise your Virtues, or your Vices blame;
Nor be displeas'd his mild Reproof to hear,
For Friends may often kindly be severe;
The Best sometimes each other may controul,
Yet not destroy the Harmony of Soul.
Rough Notes in Music never should be found,
Except adapted to improve the Sound.

When

When mutual Faith the friendly Knot has ty'd,
And when that mutual Faith is truly try'd,
Prey not upon yourself, nor be opprest
With conscious Pains that struggle in your Breast
For, as the Flames, in *Ætna* closely pent,
Convulse the Mountain, lab'ring for a Vent,
Thus in the Soul uneasy Thoughts confin'd,
For want of Passage, rack the suff'ring Mind.
Unveil your Bosom to your other Part,
Your Friend shall share the Burden of your Heart,
Alleviate ev'ry Ill your Soul sustains,
Double your Pleasures, and divide your Pains.

Be zealous for your Friends, whene'er you know
Their Reputation censur'd by a Foe,
Nor with a faint Excuse degrade your Friends,
The Man, who coldly praises, discommends.
Or, are they justly censur'd for a Crime?
Reprove them mildly at some proper Time:
In private chide all Failings which you find,
In public praise the Beauties of their Mind;
Place all their Virtues in the clearest Light,
Omit their Faults, or touch them very slight;
As Painters, when they draw a beauteous Face,
Contract a Blemish, heighten ev'ry Grace.

Neither let Passion, Pride, or private Ends,
Or changing Fortune, make you change your Friends,
Who varies oft, a faithless Temper shows,
Or, at the best, ill Judgment, when he chose.
Some Persons with themselves so disagree,
They're fix'd to nothing but Inconstancy;
With each new Day, new Resolutions come,
Expel the former, and usurp their Room:
Succeeding Billows thus the foremost throng,
Tides roll on Tides, and Waves urge Waves along.
No

Not but we may with a new Friend engage,
Before we see an old one quit the Stage;
Yet should not think the new our old exceeds,
As * Jockeys value most their youngest Steeds.
One Maxim will in Wine and Friendship hold,
Alike the better both for being old.

But must we then be bound in deathless Bands,
And still obey whate'er a Friend commands?
Aid him to gain what he unjustly craves?
No—Leave the Man, who Truth and Virtue leaves.
Should furious CATILINE some Plot devise,
To ruin Thousands, that himself might rise;
The Laws of Honour, Truth, and Conscience show,
'Tis Friendship to the World to be his Foe.
Or, should a Friend basely betray his Trust,
To pardon him were to yourself unjust.
For, † as the Wool, with Crimson colour'd o'er,
Never acquires its native Whiteness more;
So he who breaks his Faith, will ne'er obtain
Your Credit, nor his Innocence again.
If otherwise he disoblige his Friends,
(For where's the perfect Man, who ne'er offends?)
Try if his Ear will kind Reproof endure;
And, if the Balm of Counsel work a Cure,
O'erlook the Failure. All *offend*, and *live*;
Let *Foes* resent a Trespass, *Friends* forgive.

N 3   Yet

* *Ut equis vetulis teneros anteponere solemus ——————Vetustima quæque (ut ea vina, quæ vetustatem ferunt) esse debent suavissima.*
                              Cic de Amic. § 19.

† *——————Neque amissos colores
Lana refert medicata fuco;
Nec vera virtus, cum semel excidit,
Curat reponi deterioribus.*
                              Hor. Ode 5. Lib. III.

Yet let the pardon'd Friend, not many times,
Proceed in Folly, and repeat his Crimes.
Tho' pureſt Gold a vaſt Extent will bear,
Yet pureſt Gold will break if ſtretch'd too far:
And Friends may bear ſome Slips from Wiſdom's Rule;
But who can pardon the perſiſting Fool?

* Among the various Cauſes, that conſpire
To cool our Love, and quench the friendly Fire,
Vile *Avarice* aſſumes the greateſt Pow'r,
A God which baſe ignoble Souls adore.
To pleaſure him, a Tide of broken Vows
(Needful Libations!) on his Altar flows:
Yet never ſatisfy'd, he craves for more,
And keeps his Votaries, in Plenty, poor·
Who worſhips him, will break the friendly Bands,
When e'er the ſordid, ſelfiſh God commands.

Others there are, induc'd by Thirſt of Praiſe,
(And ev'n the greateſt Men this Paſſion ſways)
Who quit their Friends for Honours of the State,
And turn their Love into the rankeſt Hate.
Nor is it Wonder theſe deſert their Friends,
Since all are Foes, who will not ſerve their Ends:
For wild Ambition like a Torrent roars,
Which, when obſtructed, climbs th'oppoſing Shores;
Till to the Top the lab'ring Flood attains,
Swells o'er the Banks, and foams along the Plains.
Not but we may an honeſt Fame embrace;
Nay, Friends ſhould aid us in the glorious Chace.

Man

---

* *Peſtem enim majorem eſſe nullam in amicitiis, quam in pleriſque*
pecuniæ cupiditatem, in optimis quibuſque honoris certamen & gloriæ,
ex quo inimicitias maximas ſæpe inter amiciſſimos excitiſſe. Cic. de
Amic. § 10.

Man has some Principle of heav'nly Fire,
That warms his Breast, and prompts him to aspire;
Wakes him to Actions of superior Kind,
And keeps alive the Faculties of Mind;
For Sloth begets a Lethargy of Soul,
As want of Motion taints the clearest Pool:
Yet, if, too fond and covetous of Fame,
We blow that native Spark into a Flame,
It quickly rises to a fiery Storm,
And burns the Fabric 'twas design'd to warm.
What Bands of Nature can restrain its Course?
What friendly Offices suppress its Force?
See how its Rage the young * *Numidian* fires,
The worst of Children to the best of Sires!
Deep, thro' his Brother's Blood, he wades his Way,
And leaps o'er *Gratitude* to *Regal Sway.*
Young CÆSAR's *Tutor* by his *Pupil* dies,
While TULLY falls by him he help'd to rise;
Friends, Fathers, Brothers, Uncles, yield to Fate,
To make three *Tyrants* infamously great!

O! grant me, gracious Heav'n, where-e'er I go,
To be a faithful Friend, or gen'rous Foe;
Nor let me pant so much for empty Praise,
As to obtain it by dishonest Ways;
Nor wrong my Friend, tho' 'twere to gain a Throne;
Nor ruin others Fame to raise my own.

He who is only learn'd in Books, will find
A harder Lesson, when he learns Mankind;
A Volume gilded o'er with smiling Art,
Where few can read the Meaning of the Heart.
We often take our Flatterers for Friends;
One would suspect the Man who still commends;
Who,

* JUGURTHA,

Who, like the Sharper in the *Roman* Play,
Or right or wrong, affents to all you fay ;
Bends here or there, which way his Lord's inclin'd,
As Reeds fubmit to ev'ry diff'rent Wind.
Nor is it ftrange fuch Parafites prevail,
When greedy Ears devour the flatt'ring Tale:
While THRASO loves to hear his Praifes told,
GNATHO will *give* him *Praife,* and *take* his *Gold,*
But you, who walk by Wifdom's fafer Rules,
(For 'twere but Labour loft to counfel Fools)
Deteft the Wretch, who ne'er can Courage find
To fpeak the genuine Dictates of his Mind ,
But, like the *Syrens* fweet, pernicious Song,
At once would charm and ruin with his Tongue.

Yet fome there are, in focial Bands ally'd,
Who, with blunt Truths, err on the other Side ;
Void of Good-nature, and Good-breeding too,
They fourly cenfure every Thing you do.
O ! never flatter ev'n a Monarch's Pride,
Nor, with the Sternnefs of a *Cynic,* chide ;
But, when you would an erring Friend reprove,
Let gentle Cautions fhew, the Motive's Love:
Do not begin with Rafhnefs to exclaim ,
But rather hint the Fault, before you blame.
'Tis not enough your Admonition's juft ;
Prudence muft guide it, or the Labour's loft:
Friends fhould allure, and charm us into Senfe ;
Harfh Counfels not reform, but give Offence.
Nature, impatient of fevere Reproof,
Loves mild Inftruction, but abhors the rough:
As Fruits and Flow'rs improve with gentle Rain:
But fade, if rapid Storms o'erflow the Plain.

Some

Some Men are Friends, when Fortune fills the Sails,
And wafts you on with favourable Gales ;
But quit the tott'ring Ship, and make the Shore,
When Storms defcend, and adverfe Surges roar.
Long as in *Credit*, *Pow'r*, or *Place* you ftand,
Their fawning, formal Friendfhip you command :
With twenty *Squeezes* and a hundred *Bows*,
As many *Compliments*, as many *Vows*,
They fwear your Intereft fhall be their own,
And wifh the Time to make it better known ;
Like falfe hot Courfers, waiting for the Chace,
Which foam, and neigh, and proudly fpurn the Grafs,
Intent to run ; but droop their jaded Creft,
And fail you moft, when moft you want their Hafte.

We make a proftitute of *Friendfhip*'s Name,
It only *Complaifance* fupports our Claim.
And yet there are of this polite Degree,
Who treat you ftill with *forc'd Civility*;
In each obliging Art fo well refin'd,
Tho' ever falfe, they never feem unkind.
Not that my Mufe would Decency offend ;
For 'tis Good breeding polifhes a Friend :
Nor fhines it lefs, with *Truth* and *Virtue* join'd,
Than comely Features with a noble Mind .
But thofe, whofe Friendfhips moft in Speeches dwell,
Neglect the Fruit, and trifle with the Shell.
True Friendfhip more intrinfic Worth affords,
Defin'd by Actions better than by Words ;
A warm Affection, that can never cool,
Concord of Mind, and Mufic of the Soul ;
Which tunes the jarring Strings of Life to Love,
Shews Men below, how Angels live above.
There are in Friendfhip fuch attractive Charms,
It draws Efteem from thofe it never warms.

See

See how * PACUVIUS' tragic Scenes could move
The People's Praifes with fictitious Love !
When on the Stage two doubtful Princes ftrive,
Each feeking Death, too keep his Friend alive.
Now PYLADES deceives the Monarch's Eye,
Faithful, yet fraudulent, refolves to die:
ORESTES now difplays the friendly Cheat,
Invites the threat'ning Sword, and courts his Fate
Mov'd with their gen'rous Love, the Audience rofe,
With focial Flame each changing Bofom glows ;
All feel the facred Pow'r of Friendfhip's Laws,
And the Stage rocks, and thunders with Applaufe.

I know the Mufe may give to fome Offence,
(Tho' rather Men of Wit, than Men of Senfe)
Whofe Counfel is, " Be not engag'd too far ;
" The greateft Friendfhip brings the greateft Care·
" Our own Concerns have Plagues enough in Store ,
" Who joins in Friendfhip, only makes 'em more.
" The Cares and Troubles, which your Friend en-
      dures,
" Are all by Sympathy adopted your's."

What bafe, ungen'rous, felfifh Souls are thefe ?
Mere Quacks, who turn ev'n Health into Difeafe,
And but the darkeft Side of Friendfhip find,
To all its radiant Beams and Beauties blind.
Two faithful Friends, in any State, may gain
Comfort to heighten Joy, or leffen Pain.
If weighty Cares the penfive Mind invade,
They make the Burden light with mutual Aid ,

If

* *Qui clamores tota cavea nuper in hofpitis & amici mei M Pacu-
vii nova fabula, oum, ignorarte rege, utei eorum effet Oreftes, Pylades
Oreftem fe effe diceret, ut pro illo necaretur , Oreftes autem, ita ut erat,
Oreftem fe effe perfeveraret ? Stantes plaudebant in re ficta · quid arbi-
tramur in vera fuiffe facturos ?*

Cic. de Amic. § 7.

If Profit, or if Pleasure chears the Soul,
The Blessings common, each enjoys the Whole:
If Business calls them to some distant Place,
Swift pinion'd Love contracts the lengthen'd Space;
Each keeps the other's Image in his Breast,
As Wax preserves the Form a Seal imprest.

Hail, sacred *Friendship!* by whose chearing Ray
All Joys increase, without it fade away:
Ev'n HYMEN's *Torch*, tho' burning e'er so bright,
Aided by *Friendship*, shines with double Light.
This you, O CELIA! by Experience find,
Whose *Nuptial Friend* lives always in your Mind:
No Length of Time, no Distance, ever raz'd
His lov'd Idea from your tender Breast.
Your friendly Flame admits of no Decays,
But glows, unclouded, with augmented Rays,
And makes your bridal Lamp much brighter blaze.
That faint, pale, languid Lamp, in Age, expires;
Except 'tis fed with Friendship's constant Fires:
These to the *Winter* of our Years extend,
And, when the *Lover* cools, they warm the *Friend*.
When all the transient *Joys* of Youth are o'er,
When all the *Charms* of Beauty *charm* no more;
Surviving *Friendship* gives us fresh Supplies
Of lasting Bliss, and more substantial Joys;
Which sweeten all the Troubles Age has brought,
And make the Dregs of Life a cordial Draught.

The

The TWO BEAVERS.

A FABLE.

'TWere well, my Friend, for human kind,
 Would ev'ry Man his Bus'nefs mind,
In his own Orbit always move,
Nor blame, nor envy thofe above.

 A Beaver, well advanc'd in Age,
By long Experience render'd fage,
Was fkill'd in all the ufeful Arts,
And juftly deem'd a Beaft of Parts;
Which he apply'd (as Patriots fhou'd)
In cultivating public good.

 This Beaver on a certain Day,
A friendly Vifit went to pay
To a young Coufin pert and vain,
Who often rov'd about the Plain:
With ev'ry idle Beaft conferr'd,
Hearing, and telling what he heard.
The vagrant Youth was gone from home,
When th'ancient Sage approach'd his Dome;
Who each Apartment view'd with care,
But found each wanted much Repair.
The Walls were crack'd, decay'd the Doors,
The Corn lay mouldy on the Floors;
Thro' gaping Crannies rufh'd amain
The bluft'ring Winds, with Snow and Rain;

The

The Timber all was rotten grown, ——
In fhort, the Houfe was tumbling down.
The gen'rous Beaft, by Pity fway'd,
Griev'd to behold it thus decav'd ;
And while he mourn'd the tatter'd Scene,
The Mafter of the Lodge came in.

The firft Congratulations o'er,
They reft recumbent on the Floor ;
When thus the young conceited Beaft
His Thoughts impertinent exprefs'd.

I long have been furpriz'd to find,
The Lion grown fo wond'rous kind
To one peculiar fort of Beafts,
While he another fort detefts ,
His royal Favour chiefly falls
Upon the Species of Jack-alls.
They fhare the Profits of his Throne,
He fmiles on them, and them alone.
Mean while the Ferret's ufeful Race
He fcarce admits to fee his Face ,
Traduc'd by Lies and ill Report,
They're banifh'd from his regal Court,
And counted, over all the Plain,
Oppofers of the Lion's Reign.

Now I conceiv'd a Scheme laft Night,
Would doubtlefs fet this Matter right.
Thefe Parties fhould unite together ,
The Lion partial be to neither,
But let them both his Favours fhare,
And both confult in Peace and War.
This Method (were this Method try'd)
Would fpread politic Bafis wide,
And on a Bottom broad and ftrong,
Support the focial Union long ——

O   But

But Uncle, Uncle, much I fear,
Some have abus'd the Lion's Ear,
He liftens to the Leopard's Tongue,
That curfed Leopard leads him wrong
Were he but banifh'd far away——
You don't attend to what I fay!

Why really, Couz, the Sage rejoin'd,
The Rain and Snow, and driving Wind,
Beat thro' with fuch prodigious Force,
It made me deaf to your Difcourfe
Now, Couz, were my Advice purfu'd,
(And fure I mean it for your good)
Methinks you fhould this Houfe repair;
Be this your firft and chiefeft Care
Your Skill the Voice of Prudence calls
To ftop thefe Crannies in the Walls,
And prop the Roof before it falls.
If you this needful Tafk perform,
You'll make your Manfion dry and warm,
And we may then converfe together,
Secure from this tempeftuous Weather.

C O N T E N T M E N T.

FAREWELL afpiring Thoughts, no more
My Soul fhall leave the peaceful Shore.
  To fail Ambition's Main,
Fallacious as the Harlot's Kifs,
You promife me uncertain Blifs,
  And give me certain Pain.

A

A beauteous Prospect first you shew,
Which ere survey'd you paint anew,
  And paint it wond'rous pleasant
This in a third is quickly lost,
Thus future Good we covet most,
  But ne'er enjoy the present.

Deluded on from Scene to Scene,
We never end, but still begin,
  By flatt'ring Hope betray'd,
I'm weary of the painful Chace,
Let others run this endless Race
  To catch a flying Shade.

Let others boast their useless Wealth;
Have I not Honesty and Health?
  Which Riches cannot give
Let others to Preferment soar,
And, changing Liberty for Pow'r,
  In golden Shackles live.

Tis time, at length, I should be wise,
'Tis time to seek substantial Joys,
  Joys out of Fortunes Pow'r
Wealth, Honours, Dignities, and Fame,
Are Toys the blind capricious Dame
  Takes from us ev'ry Hour.

Come, conscious Virtue, fill my Breast,
And bring Content, thy Daughter, dress'd
  In ever-smiling Charms
Let sacred Friendship too attend,
A Friendship worthy of my Friend,
  Such as my LÆLIUS warms.

With

With thefe I'll in my Bofom make
A Bulwark Fortune cannot fhake,
   Tho' all her Storms arife,
Look down and pity gilded Slaves,
Defpife Ambition's giddy Knaves,
   And wifh the Fools were wife

On MUSIC.

MUSIC the coldeft Heart can warm,
   The hardeft melt, the fierceft charm;
Difarm the Savage of his Rage,
Difpel our Cares, and Pains afluage;
With Joy it can our Souls infpire,
And tune our Tempers to the Lyre;
Our Paffions, like the Notes agree,
And ftand fubdu'd by Harmony.
This found the *melancholy King*
When DAVID tun'd the trembling String:
Sweet Mufic chas'd the fullen Spleen away,
And made his clouded Soul ferenely gay.

II.

While Mufic breathes in martial Airs,
The Coward dares forget his Fears,
Or, if the Notes to Pity found,
Revenge and Envy ceafe to wound.
The Pow'r of Mufic has been known,
To raife or tumble Cities down
Thus *Theban* Turrets, Authors fay,
Were rais'd by Mufic's Magic Lay,

And

And antient *Jericho*'s Heav'n hated Wall,
To facred MUSIC, ow'd its deftin'd Fall.

III.

Nor Mortals only MUSIC love ;
It chears celeftial Saints above ·
Sweet Hallelujahs Angels fing
Around their great Ethereal KING ;
Ceafleſs they found the FATHER's Praife,
The FATHER too approves their Lays ,
For HE (as all Things) MUSIC made,
And SERAPHIMS before Him play'd :
When over *Horeb*'s Mount He came,
Array'd in Majefty and Flame ,
After the founding Trump, fublime, He rode ;
The founding Trump proclaim'd th' approaching
    G O D.

IV.

MUSIC had Being, long before
The folemn Organ learnt to roar .
When MICHAEL, o'er the heav'nly Plain,
Advanc'd to fight the rebel Train ,
Loud Trumpets did his Wrath declare,
In MUSIC, terrible to hear
And when the Univerfe was made.
On golden Harps the Angels play'd:
And when it falls, (as fall it muft)
MUSIC fhall penetrate the Duft ,
The Trump fhall found with the Archangel's Breath ;
And, fweetly dreadful ! wake the Dead from Death.

To a young LADY who had a CUPID given her.

FAIR Lady, take a special Care,
  This pleasing Toy become no Snare ;
The *subtle God* is full of Wiles,
And mischieves most, when most he smiles.
Beware to clasp him in your Arms,
Nor gaze too much upon his Charms ;
Lest in a borrow'd Shape he wound,
As once unhappy DIDO found ,
For while she view'd his smiling Look,
Her Heart receiv'd a fatal Stroke.

On FLORELLA's Birth Day.

THE Queen of Love, and PALLAS once, 'tis said,
  Had both agreed to form a finish'd Maid .
Upon a noted *Day* they flew to Earth,
A *Day* still noted by FLORELLA's Birth.
Both Deities employ'd their utmost Care,
To make their darling Lady wise and fair
This gave her Beauty, that a sprightly Wit,
Which render'd Soul and Body justly fit :
But MERCURY, that nimble winged Thief,
Who loves his joke, as dearly as his Life,
Down from *Olympus* to his Sisters flew,
When just to Life their little Embryo grew ;
And pour'd a little *Folly* in her Breast ;
A little *Folly* leaven'd all the rest .

Hence

Hence 'tis, she's sometime's sprightly, sometimes dull;
And sometimes witty, sometimes quite a *Fool*;
Scarce foolish now, nor witty, sprightly neither,
But sprightly, witty, foolish, all together.

PENELOPE to ULYSSES.

Paraphras'd from OVID.

THESE Lines I send, impatient of your Stay,
To you, my Lord, who kill me with Delay;
Yet crave not any Answer back, beside
Yourself, the best of Answers to your Bride
Sure *Troy*, so hateful to the *Grecian* Dames,
Is ruin'd now, with dire, consuming Flames;
Tho' scarcely *Troy*, nor all his King could boast,
Was Worth the Trouble which her Ruin cost
O! had lewd PARIS sunk beneath the Tide,
When, o'er the Seas, he sought the *Spartan* Bride;
I had not then accus'd the ling'ring Day,
Nor weav'd to charm the tedious Night away,
Nor in the Bed, deserted and forlorn,
Lain weeping, cold and comfortless till Morn.

Whene'er

Whene'er of Dangers in your Camp I heard,
Those Dangers threaten'd *you*, I always fear'd .
For Love, like mine, no cold Indiff'rence bears ;
It feeds on tim'rous Thoughts, and anxious Cares.
I fancy'd, furious *Trojans* round thee came ;
And trembling, ever dreaded HECTOR's Name ;
If any said, ANTILOCHUS was slain,
ANTILOCHUS was he who caus'd my Pain .
Or, if in borrow'd Arms PATROCLUS bled,
I wept, because his Craft no better sped .
When *Rhodian* Blood had bath'd the *Lycian* Spear,
The *Rhodian* * Youth again renew'd my Care,
In fine, whatever *Grecian* Chief was kill'd,
My fearful Heart, like frigid Ice, was chill'd ;
Lest flatt'ring Fame my doubtful Ears should cheat,
And, for my Lords proclaim another's Fate :
But Heav'n, propitious to my chaste Desire,
Preserv'd you safe, and *Troy* consum'd with Fire.

But now the other *Grecian* Chiefs return,
And on their smoking Altars Off'rings burn ,
Their useless Arms they consecrate to Peace,
And *Trojan* Spoils the *Grecian* Temples grace :
Each youthful Bride some pleasing Gift affords,
To welcome home their safe-returned Lords ;
Their safe returned Lords, in Songs of Joy,
Resound the vanquish'd Fates of ruin'd *Troy*
The wond'ring Sages croud around to hear ;
The trembling Girls admire the Tales of War .
The Wives stand list'ning, while their Husbands tell,
How *Greece* had conquer'd, and how *Ilion* fell ·
One stains a Table with the purple Draught,
And shews the furious Battles, which you fought .

* TLEPOLEMUS.

Paints

Paints with the Wine, which from the Glass he pours,
Camps, Rivers, Hills, and all the *Trojan* Tow'rs.
And, This, says he, is the *Sigean* Plain,
And here the silver *Simois* rolls his Train;
There stood old PRIAM's stately Palace, here
ACHILLES pitch'd his Tent, ULYSSES there,
Here mang'ed HECTOR, dreadful in his Fall,
Affrights the Steeds, that drag him round the Wall.
Your Son, who sent by me to NESTOR's Court,
To seek his Father, brought me this Report
From NESTOR's Mouth, and how the *Thracian* Lord,
In Sleep became a Victim to your Sword,
How DOLON fell into your crafty Snare ———
But, O! ULYSSES, you too boldly dare,
Too fearless, thro' the Camp of Foes you rove,
Mindful of Wiles, forgetful of your Love;
Slaying so many in a gloomy Night,
One Friend alone, to aid you in the Fight.
It was not thus you rashly us'd to go
Among the Midnight Terrors of the Foe;
Fondly of me you formerly have thought,
With Prudence acted, and with Caution fought.
Heav'n knows, with Fear my trembling Bosom beat,
To hear my Son your daring Deeds relate,
Till told how you victoriously return'd,
Safe, to your Camp, with *Thracian* Spoils adorn'd.

But what avails it me, your Arms have thrown
Troy's stately Walls, and lofty Turrets down?
As when they stood, if I am robb'd of thee,
Troy's fall'n to *others*, standing still to *me*,
To *others*, who, with captive Oxen, toil
To turn the Glebe, and till the *Trojan* Soil;
And while, with crooked Ploughs, they discompose
Th' ill bury'd Ashes of their slaughter'd Foes,
While *Phrygian* Fields, grown fat with native Blood,
Bear fruitful Crops, where stately *Ilion* stood;

While

While verdant Harvefts h·de their ruin'd Wall,
I mourn my abfent Lord, who wrought its Fall,
Nor can I know the Land, where you refide,
Nor who, nor what detains you from your Bride.

Whatever Sailors on our Coaft appear,
(Hopeful to find fome Tidings of my Dear)
I fly to them, and afk 'em o'er and o'er,
If e'er they faw you on fome foreign Shore.
Then to their Hands, a Letter I impart,
To give it you the Partner of my Heart;
If Chance, or Deftiny fhould ever prove
So kind to lead them to my abfent Love.

We fought for you at antient NESTOR's Court;
But fought in vain, we heard no true Report.
We fent to afk the *Spartans* too, but they
Knew not the Climate, where you, ling'ring ftay.
O! had APOLLO fav'd his facred Town ——
Ye Gods! why did I ever wifh it down?
If *that* were ftanding and ULYSSES there,
I nothing, but the Chance of War, fhould fear:
I fhould not then be fingly curs'd to cry,
Others would fear the War, no lefs than I
But now a thoufand Whimfies feed my Care,
Nor know I what to hope, or what to fear,
Yet fearing all, that Fancy can fuggeft,
Unnumber'd Troubles rack my anxious Breaft.
Upon the Land whatever Dangers reign,
I fear thofe Dangers make you there remain;
Upon the Seas whatever Storms increafe,
I fear thofe Storms detain you on the Seas.
While thus my foolifh Thoughts uncertain rove,
Perhaps you revel with a foreign Love;
Perhaps you ridicule your Bride at home,
Tell how fhe fpins, or drudges in the Loom:

Suspicious Thoughts ! that vex my jealous Mind,
Be gone, and vanish into empty Wind !
If cruel Fate did not obstruct the Way,
My Lord would never make so long Delay.
Your long Delay my Father often blames,
And often chides me for my constant Flames
My constant Flames shall ever true remain ;
Let Fathers chide, and Suiters court in vain:
At length my Sire, who finds he can't remove
My Faith from you, or shake my settled Love,
Remits his Anger, soften'd with my Pray'rs,
Yet still a Croud of Suiters teaze my Ears ;
From various Realms they come to seek your Crown,
And feast, and reign securely in your Throne ·
'Twould tire me ev'n to count their Number o'er,
MEDON, PISANDER, and a hundred more !
All bent on Love, and Robbers of the State,
And All, by your pernicious Absence, great !
To crown your Shame, the Beggar IRUS preys
Upon your Sheep, and all the fattest slays
And ev'n your Shepherd, faithless to his Lord,
Slaughters your Lambs, to grace the Suiters Board.
Nor have we Strength, their Rapine to oppose,
For how can Three resist so many Foes?
Your feeble Wife, your Father worn with Age,
Your tender Son too weak to check their Rage,
For whom they lately crafty Ambush laid,
And menac'd Death on his devoted Head,
When, mocking all their Stratagems, he crost
The Seas, to seek you on the *Pylian* Coast.
O ! may the Gods extend his vital Date,
And guard his Life, till ours submit to Fate.
So may he close our Eyes with decent Care ;
Such is your Servant's, such his Nurse's Pray'r.

Since

Since then your aged Father, feeble grown,
Amidst your Foes, cannot defend your Crown;
Your Wife, too weak to chafe the Foes away,
Your Son, too young to bear the Regal Sway;
Hafte, hafte, ULYSSES, to your Royal Seat;
For you alone can cure our troubled State ·
Think of your Son, who wants you to infpire
His Soul with all the Virtues of his Sire ·
Think, on the Brink of Fate your Father lies:
Return, my Lord, return, and clofe his Eyes
Think of your faithful Wife, whofe youthful Face,
At your Departure, blufh'd with blooming Grace:
But now I blufh with bloomy Grace no more,
Tears, for your Abfence, cloud my Beauty o'er.
O ! may you foon return, before I prove
An antient Dame, unworthy of your *Love.*

F I N I S.

Lightning Source UK Ltd.
Milton Keynes UK
176349UK00004B/18/P

9 781170 480571